MONSIGNOR WILLIAM BARRY MEMORIAL LIBRARY
BARRY UNIVERSITY

Q1603 .C3
ameron, Keith C.   010101 000
grippa d'Aubigne / by Keith C

0 2210 0060953 9

Y0-CJG-009

PQ
1603
.C3

107463

Msgr. Wm. Barry Memorial Library
Barry College
Miami, FL 33161

CAMERON

AGRIPPA D'AUBIGNE

TWAYNE'S WORLD AUTHORS SERIES

A Survey of the World's Literature

Sylvia E. Bowman, Indiana University
GENERAL EDITOR

FRANCE

Maxwell A. Smith, Guerry Professor of French, Emeritus
The University of Chattanooga
Former Visiting Professor in Modern Languages
The Florida State University

EDITOR

Agrippa d'Aubigné

TWAS 443

Agrippa D'Aubigné

AGRIPPA D'AUBIGNÉ

By KEITH CAMERON

University of Exeter
Exeter, Great Britain

TWAYNE PUBLISHERS
A DIVISION OF G. K. HALL & CO., BOSTON

Copyright © 1977 by G.K. Hall & Co.
All Rights Reserved
First Printing

Library of Congress Cataloging in Publication Data

Cameron, Keith C
　Agrippa d'Aubigné.

(Twayne's world authors series; TWAS 443: France)
Bibliography: p. 165-66.
Includes index.
1. Aubigné, Théodore Agrippa d', 1552-1630.
2. Authors, French—16th century—Biography.
PQ1603.C3   841'.3   77-540
ISBN 0-8057-6280-9

MANUFACTURED IN THE UNITED STATES OF AMERICA

Contents

About the Author
Preface
Chronology

1.	The Soldier-Author	11
2.	*Le Printemps*	17
3.	A Poetic Vision—*Les Tragiques*	38
4.	The Novelist	82
5.	The Satirist	104
6.	The King and the People	121
7.	"The Meditations on the Psalms"	128
8.	A Poet of Many Parts	138
9.	Conclusion	154
	Notes and References	157
	Selected Bibliography	165
	Index	167

About the Author

Keith C. Cameron is Senior Lecturer in French at the University of Exeter where he has been a member of the faculty since 1966. Previously he was an Assistant Lecturer in French at the University of Aberdeen. Publications, apart from articles in learned journals, on aspects of sixteenth century literature and civilization include *Montaigne et l'humour,* Minard, Paris 1966; and editions of French sixteenth century tragedy, Th. de Bèze, *Abraham Sacrifiant,* Droz, Geneva 1967; Rivaudeau, *Aman,* Droz, Geneva 1969; Chantelouve, *La Tragedie de feu Gaspard de Colligny,* Exeter Textes littéraires 1971. Since 1970 he has also been General Editor of Textes littéraires published by the University of Exeter, and Director and General Editor of Tapes on Aspects of Literature published as Exeter Tapes by the same University.

Preface

Little time is needed when undertaking an examination of the works of Agrippa d'Aubigné to realize the magnitude of the task, for the variety of his output bears witness to the manifold interests of this polymath, fearless Huguenot and distinguished soldier. I have not been able, within the limits imposed by the format of the series, to do full justice to the author's genius, and it has been necessary to restrict my study to the works in French which can be loosely described as "general literature." Lack of space prevented my treating the author's considerable correspondence, and the *Histoire universelle,* which forms an important part of d'Aubigné's lifework, has had to be omitted, as belonging to a genre which was beyond my competence to appraise. I have also omitted *L'Enfer,* which can only be vaguely attributed to our author. Quotations are taken from the Réaume and Caussade edition and also wherever possible, from the Weber edition of the *Oeuvres.*

The aim of the book is to bring the author to the attention of a greater number of general readers and to provide an introduction for the professional student of sixteenth-century literature. In the study of d'Aubigné's work, in view of the difficulty in obtaining editions of all the texts, emphasis has been laid upon the actual content and the background of the literature, thereby restricting the critical appraisal, but it is hoped that such an approach will encourage the reader to seek out the original whenever this is possible. Although translations have been provided the quotations are given generally in the original French, as so much of the poetry is lost in the transposition.

Finally, may I express here my thanks to the University of Exeter for its help toward my research expenses, to my colleagues Dr. D. Watts and Dr. J. D. Biard for their help and patience in reading through my manuscript, and also to Mrs. Lynn Spiller for her excellent secretarial assistance.

KEITH CAMERON

University of Exeter

Chronology

1552 February 8, Theodore Agrippa d'Aubigné born in the "Hostel Saint-Maury" near Pons.
1556 Begins to receive instruction in Latin, Greek, Hebrew, and French.
1559 Translates with Jean Morel's help the Socratic dialogue, *Crito; or, The Duty of a Citizen.*
1560 March–April, Agrippa is taken by his father to Paris via Amboise.
1562 Goes to Paris to study with Mathieu Béroald. Takes refuge in the Protestant stronghold of Orléans. Catches the plague.
1565 Sent to study in Geneva.
1566 Leaves Geneva for Lyons. Initiated into the occult sciences.
1567 D'Aubigné returns to the Saintonge shortly after the outbreak of the second War of Religion.
1568 Enters the duke of Asnières's company.
1569 Participates in the battles of Jarnac, Moncontour, and La Roche-Abeille.
1570 Falls in love with Diane Salviati. He composes in her honor many of the poems in *Le Printemps.*
1572 Escapes the Massacre of St. Bartholomew's Day because he is obliged to leave Paris three days earlier on August 21 after wounding a sergeant in a duel. D'Aubigné is attacked and seriously wounded and is tended by Diane de Talcy.
1573 Begins to compose the *Stances.* Appointed equerry to Henry of Navarre.
1574 Sent by Henry of Navarre to support the Catholic forces against Mongommery in Normandy.
1575 Produces a number of poems, of a satirical, eulogious, and circumstantial nature.
1577 Writes first lines of *Les Tragiques;* composes *Elégie autobiographique.*
1578 Continues composition of *Les Tragiques.*
1586 Begins to study Catholic theologians and becomes an even more convinced Protestant.
1589 D'Aubigné nominated governor of Maillezais.

1600 D'Aubigné tricked into semi-public dispute with Du Perron. Writes *Lettre à Madame sur la Douceur des Afflictions*. Begins to write the *Histoire universelle*.
1612 Writes *Le Caducée ou l'Ange de la Paix*.
1616 Publishes anonymously *Les Tragiques*.
1617 Begins to write the *Avantures du Baron de Faeneste* of which the first two volumes are published the same year.
1618 Publishes first volume of the *Histoire universelle*.
1619 Publishes Book 3 of *Avantures du baron de Faeneste* and Volume 2 of the *Histoire universelle,* without a royal privilege.
1620 The *Histoire universelle* is condemned to be burned and d'Aubigné summoned to defend himself at the Châtelet. In danger of his life he has to flee the country. Arrives in Geneva.
1621 Composes two pamphlets against Luynes: "Lettre au Roy" and "A Messeigneurs Les Grands du Royaume." Writes the *Traitté sur les Guerres Civiles* and the treatise, *Debvoir mutuel des Roys et des subjects*.
1626 *Histoire universelle* published. Composes *La Création* and *Sa vie à ses enfants*.
1630 Publishes the *Petites Oeuvres meslées* and the fourth book of the *Avantures du baron de Faeneste*. D'Aubigné dies on May 8.

CHAPTER 1

The Soldier-Author

AGRIPPA d'Aubigné's life mirrored the troubled times in which he lived, and it was as varied and chequered as his literary output. It spans one of the most turbulent periods not only in the history of France, but indeed, in that of Western Europe. The conflicts raised by the opposition of the feudal and capitalist systems were exacerbated by the struggle between Catholics and Protestants. France, after the death of Henry II in 1559, had a succession of weak kings. Civil war was constantly breaking out, and it took the death of many and the firm hand of Henry IV to reestablish some sort of peace. It took even longer to quiet all the differences which existed between the Huguenot and the Catholic factions, differences which were often political and social as well as religious. If one man, so Sainte-Beuve claims, can be said to represent an epoch, then that man is Agrippa d'Aubigné.

I *A Huguenot Education*

There is something of the romantic hero about Agrippa for, like many of them, he was not to know a mother's affection. As his name recalls (Agrippa - aegre partus), his mother died while giving birth to him. His father, Jean d'Aubigné, was a committed Protestant and brought his son up to be a staunch and unyielding supporter of that faith. When travelling with his father through Amboise on his way to Paris in 1560, the eight-year-old boy was made to swear to avenge those Protestants whose bodies were still hanging in front of the castle, after having been found guilty of treason in the conspiracy of Amboise.

Both as a child and as an adult he was always to feel on the edge of society and he was never able to accept any political compromise which, in his view, weakened the position of the Huguenots; he continued to wage his own personal battle against the State long after certain issues had, in the opinion of many, been resolved.

When his father remarried, he was raised outside his father's household by Michelle Jolly, his cousin, first at Archiac and then in the house of Antoinette d'Albret in Pons, where he met and began his life-long association with the future Henry IV. His education was first entrusted to private tutors, the fervent anti-Catholic, Jean Cottin and later, a certain Peregim. He received instruction in Latin, Greek, Hebrew and French and he claims to have been proficient in these by the age of six. Another tutor, Jean Morel, showed the child great consideration and it was under his guidance that Agrippa translated the Socratic dialogue, *Crito; or, The Duty of a Citizen.* It was at this time that an event occurred which illustrates the boy's hyper-sensitive imagination, something he was to have all his life. He maintains that he had a vision during which the very pale figure of a woman approached him and, with icy lips, kissed him on the brow. He was so overcome that he lost the use of speech and fell into a fortnight-long feverish state. Such a strong physical reaction to an emotional experience seems to have been a feature of his existence and was to recur relatively frequently. On the first occasion, however, he may well have been influenced by the Socratic text he had been studying with Morel, for in the *Crito,* Socrates also has a vision of a beautiful and majestic woman, clad in white garments, who spoke with him.

At the age of ten he was sent to study under the esteemed Matthieu Béroald in Paris and followed him to Orléans when the Protestants were expelled from Paris in May, 1562. The next year, Orléans was besieged and Agrippa's father came to negotiate a peace with the Queen Mother. It was the boy's first experience of war and he was greatly affected by the death of his father who, after the conclusion of peace, passed away as a result of a wound received at Amboise.

His guardians decided in favour of a more formal education and in 1565 he arrived in Geneva. In this bastion of Huguenot faith and culture, Agrippa's advanced learning was not respected and he was made to sit on the school benches. With adolescent pique he reacted against his studies and became dissipated, still finding time, however, to write some Latin verse. His departure for Lyons the following year is surrounded in mystery but it was probably a consequence of his having been the victim of a homosexual approach from a fellow school-boy, Bartolomé Tecia. This affair no doubt left a profound impression on d'Aubigné for when the boy's practices became known, Tecia was condemned to be drowned in the Rhone for his sins.

In Lyons, he was introduced to the occult sciences by a bogus scholar, Loys d'Arza; these sciences no doubt helped to confirm his deep belief in and suspicion of the diabolic presence in the world. It was while in Lyons that Agrippa knew the anguish of poverty and solitude and was, so he claims, contemplating suicide when a messenger arrived bearing money from his guardian — obviously a miraculous example of divine intervention. His formal education was now complete and he returned to his home, a young man versed in the humanities, convinced in his faith, and determined to defend the Protestant cause.

II *An Active Life*

The 1560's were years of bloodshed, of peace treaties and fresh outbreaks of war. In the duke of Asnière's company, the young d'Aubigné gained a varied experience of military life. As he rose from standard-bearer to the rank of general, he took a very active part in battles and skirmishes, and was wounded on several occasions.

War in the sixteenth-century was not an all-season affair and there was ample opportunity for the noble warrior to pursue his ill-fated romance with Diane de Talcy. He also became an equerry in the King of Navarre's suite during the latter's enforced stay in the French capital after the St. Bartholomew's Day Massacre in August, 1572. His observation of court life, both in Paris and later, in the Navarre courts of Pau and Nérac, provided him with much of the material for his satirical and circumstantial literary works.

D'Aubigné's relationship with Henry IV as a member of his suite or as a royal intermediary, was not an ordinary king-subject one. In his autobiography, Agrippa stresses his own independence of outlook and how he would often remonstrate with the king when he disagreed with his sovereign's behavior. Such outspoken criticism often incurred the king's resentment, as did d'Aubigné's reception of Henry in Oléron in 1586. D'Aubigné had captured the island and had become its governor. The display of magnificence he provided when he received Henry had an effect upon him similar to that of the reception offered by Fouquet to Louis XIV at Vaux-le-Vicomte seven decades later. The king did not come to d'Aubigné's rescue when the island was recaptured by St Luc later the same year and its proud governor was taken prisoner. And yet, by the following year, d'Aubigné and Navarre had made up their differences — such was the pattern of their love-hate behavior.

When, in 1589, he became governor of the town of Maillezais in the Vendée, he proceeded to consider it as his own private capital. It was with great bitterness that d'Aubigné witnessed the king's abjuration and acceptance of the Catholic faith in 1593. He felt that Henry had betrayed the Protestants and was to remain suspicious of him ever afterwards. He refused to accept the terms of the Edict of Nantes in 1598, being of the opinion that the Protestants had once more been denied their full rights. He became a leading figure in Protestant assemblies and still visited the court where he did not miss an opportunity of slating leading representatives of Catholicism, such as the Cardinal Du Perron and the king's confessor, Father Cotton.

Grief-stricken by Henry's assassination in 1610 by Ravaillac, d'Aubigné interpreted it as an act of God. During the years of Marie de Medici's regency he became more and more dissatisfied with his position and with that of the Protestants. He believed that certain people were compromising Protestant principles by submitting to royal will. He undertook the construction of a private fortress at Dognon, near Maillezais and, after supporting Condé in his opposition to the King in 1615, he lost his royal pension.

The pen now became as important as the sword to him, and he published *Les Tragiques,* the *Avantures du baron de Faeneste,* and the *Histoire universelle.* These publications aroused more enmity than support, and their author appears to have become more and more embittered against the ruling party.

His private life had not been more satisfying. Suzanne de Lezay, whom he had married in 1583, had died in 1595. Of his children, his son Constant, the father of Mme de Maintenon, was to be a continual source of shame to him. Constant had made a mésalliance by marrying a poor nobleman's widow, a woman of doubtful reputation, from La Rochelle in 1608, and he had later consorted with the Catholics. He even went so far as to attack his father at Maillezais in 1619.

When the *Histoire universelle* was condemned to be burned in 1620, the author was summoned to defend himself at the Châtelet; he also became involved in the revolt against Luynes in the same year. In danger of his life, d'Aubigné was forced to flee the country and take refuge in Geneva.

The Soldier-Author

Until his death, Geneva was to remain his home. This energetic man of almost seventy did not associate exile with retirement. D'Aubigné devoted himself to the Protestant cause with his customary fervor, assuming the role of a military adviser to Geneva, Berne, and Bâle, and offered his services to those princes who fought in the name of Protestantism. He even married again. Renée Burlamachi, a fifty-eight-year-old widow became his wife in 1623. They lived in a fortified house, the Château du Crest, just outside of Geneva. With him also was his natural son, Nathan de la Fosse (born 1600), whose birth bears witness to another aspect of sixteenth-century mores. D'Aubigné does not seem to have been ashamed of his behavior in spite of his usual excessive hatred of sin. He was, in all senses of the term, an outstanding individual, a mixture of coarseness and sophistication, of piety and bloodthirstiness and yet, always a man of learning and of great determination, a seeker and a fighter. His death, in 1630, coincided with the destruction of the military and political power of the Protestants in France; his life had paralleled the rise and fall of Protestant resistance, both armed and polemical, to Catholic oppression. With him expired the spirit of a whole epoch, a spirit which we can recapture to a certain extent through the passion and dynamism of his writing.

III *The Manuscripts*

From Geneva, d'Aubigné carried on a frequent and varied correspondence with important dignitaries of his day on a host of topics. He also continued to write creatively, but much of his literary output was not published until many years after his death. The manuscripts are now in the Bibliothèque Publique et Universitaire of Geneva.[1] On his death, d'Aubigné nominated as his literary heirs, his illegitimate son, Nathan d'Aubigné de la Fosse, and Dr. Théodore Tronchin (1582–1657) who, born into a Genevan bourgeois family, and a godson of Théodore de Bèze, was appointed in 1615 to the chair of theology once held by Calvin and was thus the most important theologian in Geneva at the time of d'Aubigné's stay there. D'Aubigné, as he reveals in his correspondence, had a great affection for Tronchin, saying that "je ne m'ayme pas tant que je croy estre aymé de luy".[2]

The manuscripts remained in the hands of the Tronchin family until this century when they were bequeathed to the Geneva library.

They form a weighty compendium of d'Aubignalia and are written in a number of different hands. D'Aubigné in his will had exhorted his literary executors to *ure et seca* ("to burn and to cut"), and the extent to which they followed his advice has yet to be measured. The author had already used the same phrase when writing to Simon Gouiard in 1616 about *Les Tragiques*,[3] revealing perhaps his own realization of his hyperbolic tendencies and his need for an Aristarchus.

Several versions of some of his works are contained in the manuscripts, and the variants afford an interesting insight into the formation of d'Aubigné's ideas and style. The script is not always perfectly legible and the print-through on certain pages does not allow an easy reading of all the texts. It would doubtless be a worthwhile venture to reprint the whole of d'Aubigné's works in the light of modern scholarship and thus make readily accessible an edition which would supersede the meritorious one prepared by Réaume and Caussade and supplement the otherwise excellent partial edition of d'Aubigné's *Oeuvres* established in recent years by H. Weber, J. Bailbé, and M. Soulié.

CHAPTER 2

Le Printemps

I *The Collection*

THE poems which form the collection, called by d'Aubigné himself *La Jeunesse,* and later *Le Printemps,* were not published before the nineteenth century. They represent some of his earliest poetic endeavors and the manuscripts have three divisions: the *Hécatombe à Diane* (sonnets), the *Stances,* and the *Odes.* D'Aubigné is rather laconic about the circumstances surrounding their composition:

D'Aubigné devint amoureux de Diane Salviaty, fille aisnee de Talcy. Cet amour luy mit en teste la poësie françoise, et lors il composa ce que nous appelons son *Printems,* où il y a plusieurs choses moins polies, mais quelque fureur qui sera au gré de plusieurs.[1]

D'Aubigné fell in love with Diane Salviaty, oldest daughter of the Lord of Talcy. That brought to his mind French poetry, and then he composed what we call his *Printemps,* which contains several poems lacking in polish, but a certain fury of inspiration which will be to the liking of some.

Diane Salviati, niece of Ronsard's Cassandra, was the daughter of Jean Salviati, member of a rich banking family of Florentine origin and who owned Talcy, a property situated close to d'Aubigné's own Château des Landes-Guinemer in the Loire valley between Orléans and Blois. If we are to believe the poet, Diane was the source of an overpowering passion in 1571 and the following year. He sought her out in marriage and at first his suit seems to have been received favorably. It was to Talcy that the impetuous young Agrippa repaired in 1572 to seek protection when pursued by Catholic forces after the Massacre of St. Bartholomew's Day. Was it out of sympathy for the young Huguenot suitor or for more sinister reasons that Jean Salviati, a powerful member of the household of the duchess of Lorraine, afforded him a refuge? In his autobiography, d'Aubigné reveals what may have been Salviati's attempt to involve him in espionage by suggesting that he could blackmail the former chancellor, Michel de l'Hospital, with papers he still had in his possession from the Conspiracy of Amboise (1559). Whatever Salviati's intentions may have been, d'Aubigné's reaction was typical, given his fiery personality. As soon as Diane's father had spoken with him, Agrippa rushed to get the documents and throw them into the fire so that "they should burn rather than burn him, for he had been tempted." The next day, the lord of Talcy promised his daughter to d'Aubigné because his great probity had made a very favorable impression upon him. Shortly afterward the soldier-poet was severely wounded in an attack as he was leaving an inn in the Beauce. Once more he returned to Talcy and was restored to health under Diane's care:

> En portant avecq' moy ma fin j'ay traversee
> La Beausse presque entier, et mon ame pressee
> Pressa le cors d'aller, de vivre et de courir
> Pour entre ses doux bras si doucement mourir[2]

And bearing my death with me I crossed almost the whole of the Beauce, and my hard-pressed soul pressed my body on to live and to rush so as to die such a sweet death in her sweet arms.

Later that same year the promise of marriage was broken through the intervention of Diane's uncle, the Chevalier Salviati, on religious grounds. D'Aubigné's tone in the poems and his continued accusation of unfaithfulness and inconstancy leveled at Diane, would suggest, however, that his beloved's role in the breakdown of the projected marriage had not been negligible.

The young man was violently affected by the breaking off of the engagement. He fell so ill that doctors from Paris had to be called to treat him. His wounds of love, as is so often the case, gradually healed and when he next mentions Diane it is at a court tournament a couple of years later. According to him, Mademoiselle Salviati, betrothed then to a certain Limeux, on realizing the difference between the man she had and the one she had lost, was so distraught, so stricken with melancholia, that her health suffered and she died of grief.

Le Printemps

Thus we have a powerfully realistic background for a colleetion of love poems — youth, beauty, a wounded, later rejected suitor, death through langor, etc. It was by a conscious mental association that the author entitled his set of poems *Le Printemps* in order to record the fact that they emanated from the spring years of his life. The collective title also contrasts with that of the poems written toward the end of his long career (and entitled *L'Hiver*). Not all the poems were composed, as one might expect, during the years of his courtship of Diane (1571-1573). A number of the *Stances* and many of the *Odes* were written not for Diane but for members of the court at Pau and Nérac, where d'Aubigné was often in the company of the future Henri IV and the queen of Navarre, Marguerite de Valois, between 1579 and 1582. In subsequent years, the poet deprecated his earlier outpourings on a theme of profane love, and in the preface and opening lines of *Les Tragiques* he spurns and denounces "les feux d'un amour inconu" (T,I, 1.55). One might consider this to be a Protestant literary pattern, for other Protestants who had tried their hand at love poetry before turning to religious verse had also experienced a guilt similar to that of d'Aubigné in the face of their youthful enthusiasm and passion. For example, Théodore de Bèze in his "Avis aux lecteurs" introducing the first tragedy written in French, *Abraham Sacrifiant* (1550), apologized for his literary peccadilloes "en choses desquelles la seule souvenance [le] fait rougir." Similarly Jean de Boyssières prefaces a section of religious verse in his *Troisiesmes Oeuvres* (1579), with a poem, "A Dieu," which begins:

> Si j'ay oublié tes services,
> Pour vivre entre un millier de vices,
> Bandé de plaisantes fureurs.
> Et si comme les Escrevices,
> J'ay cherché toutes immondices,
> Et cheminé dans les erreurs.
> Helas! Seigneur plein de clemence,
> Ores tu vois que je commence
> D'avoir les maux en mille horreurs.

If I have forgotten your services, to live amid a thousand vices, blinded by pleasing furies; and if like the crayfish, I have sought out all the filth, and wandered in error; Alas, Oh Lord full of mercy, now you can see that I am beginning to look with great horror on evil things.

We might also mention Pierre Poupo who in his *La Muse Chrestienne* (1590) repeats the same sentiments. And yet, for the majority of these Protestants, contemporaries of d'Aubigné, their love poetry possesses a quite different tone from that of *Le Printemps*. They tend to reveal the influence of Ronsard in the rhythms and forms they use, but to avoid his lasciviousness and "mignardise";[3] they try and reconcile their love for a woman with their love for God. The love experienced by d'Aubigné was too passionate for him to subject it to God, and this may explain why the poems were never published during his lifetime and why he harbored such a strong sense of guilt about them, once he became fully committed to the Protestant cause. For as Théodore de Bèze considered his *Juvenilia* to be unworthy of a man of the church, so Agrippa d'Aubigné repudiated *Le Printemps* as being incompatible with the role of soldier-poet he later assumed in *Les Tragiques*.

The sincerity of the passion that d'Aubigné had for Diane cannot be questioned. Even after his marriage to Suzanne de Lezay he would cry out for Diane during his sleep — as he writes in a sonnet composed to explain this fact to his wife: "Pourquoy ne peut sa mort me donner de l'amour/Puisque morte elle peut te donner jalousie?" (*PD,* p. 51) ("Why can her death not give me love, since dead she can make you jealous?"). We could therefore conjecture that d'Aubigné had something of an advantage over contemporary poets such as Ronsard and Desportes, to whom he owes a great deal for the form and the style. He was able to write poetry using the conventions of the day, but twisting them to reflect the intensity and the idiosyncratic nature of his own amorous experiences.

II L'Hécatombe à Diane

The sixteenth-century poets often chose or bestowed upon the object of their amatory verse a name rich in evocative value — Cassandre, Marie, Astrée, Héléne, Olive, Olimpe, Délie: and, in 1573, Desportes had published his own *Amours de Diane*. D'Aubigné does not let slip the opportunity of making full use of Diane's name and of all its connotations. The collection of one hundred sonnets reflects the association between Hecate, one of the Greek names for Diana in Hades, and the Greek homophone meaning one hundred. They represent his sacrifice to try and appease his beloved, as in Greek religious mythology Hecate/Diana had demanded a sacrifice of a hundred bulls:

Le Printemps

> Pour ces justes raisons, j'ay observé les cent:
> A moins de cent taureaux on ne fait cesser l'ire
> De Diane en courrous, et Diane retire
> Cent ans hors de l'enfer les corps sans monument.
>
> (*PR*, 96)

For these very reasons I have respected the hundred: with less than a hundred bulls you do not stop the ire of angry Diana and Diana keeps out from Hades for a hundred years the bodies without a tomb.

Elsewhere he recalls the image of Diana the huntress (*PR*, 21), longs for the pleasures given to Endymion by the goddess (Il fust aimé, et je ne suis qu'amy" [*PR*, 37]), and develops Diana's heavenly connection with the moon ("Tu es l'astre du froid et des humiditez" [*PR*, 88]).

In his preface, the poet speaks tenderly of his paternal feelings of affection for the collection which is the child of his spirit. Contrary to contemporary custom, d'Aubigné avoids dedicating his work to a great man; this is an act of independence and freedom, showing his scorn for the help of the powerful: "Livre, celuy qui te donne/N'est esclave de personne" (*PR*, ll. 31-32). ("Oh book, he who offers you is the slave of no man.)

Three or four years before beginning the sonnets, d'Aubigné, at the age of sixteen, had composed a number of lines in honor of Ronsard: "Je n'entans que Ronsard, Ronsard et sa louange" (*PD*, p. 207). (I hear but Ronsard, Ronsard and his praises). There is no doubt that the influence of Ronsard over the young man's style and poetic method is important.[4] His aversion for the common herd, "le vulgaire," is reminiscent of that of the Pléiade. He is enflamed, for example, at the idea that the name Diane should be sullied by being pronounced by the profane:

> J'enrage que ma Diane
> Passe en la bouche prophane
> Du vulgaire sans renom.
>
> (*PR*, preface, 85-87)

I am enflamed that my Diane should pass into the profane mouth of the unknown populace.

But like the experienced Ronsard, the author of the *Amours de Marie*, d'Aubigné realizes the dangers of esotericism, of obscure expression:

> Et vault beaucoup mieux se faire
> Bien entendre qu'admirer.
> Ces periphrases obscures
> Sont subjectes aux injures....
>
> (*PR*, ll. 95–98)

It is highly preferable to be well understood than admired. These obscure periphrases are subject to insults.

Similarly, he does not hide his scorn for the fawning, affected courtiers, "Tous les singes de la cour" (*PR*, l.150), who could hardly be considered to be qualified judges of his poetry. This fairly traditional attack on court taste is developed with an ironical outburst against those soldiers of the monster Ignorance, who, in medieval fashion, seek the ruin of virtue; and the preface ends with a dig at envious, but obscure, poetasters.

III The Poet's Sincerity

In a hundred sonnets the poet expresses the whole gamut of love emotions: the suffering, the joys, and the tribulations of a man whose heart has been stolen by a charming girl in her teens. By the sheer intensity of his language he gives an overpowering impression of sincerity, yet we cannot attach too much importance to this fact. Beneath the violent, passionate surface of the verse we find a definite Petrarchist infrastructure. So many of the themes developed by d'Aubigné had known, and were to know still, a great vogue in the love poetry of the sixteenth century. The influence of Petrarch and the Petrarchist Italian authors is clearly visible.[5] Petrarch and his imitators had evolved and enunciated a poetic quintessence of the language of love. Within the growing sophistication of the Italian courts of the *Quattrocento* and the French ones of the sixteenth century, the Petrarchist themes abounded and were used and used again to win the favor of the poet's beloved. Many poets espoused the words without sharing the sentiments they expressed. Did Ronsard really love Cassandra? or Marie? or Hélène? Such questions provide the substance for academic arguments but have little bearing on the quality of the poetry itself. What is all-important is the degree of sincerity the poet succeeds in conveying through his subtle, evocative use of themes and words. That d'Aubigné loved Diane is a fact; that he was also conscious of writing in an estab-

Le Printemps

lished literary tradition is another. One of the charms for d'Aubigné in singing the praises of Diane Salviati in verse is that of having a sense of continuing a poetic vein: for Ronsard had already, in a highly stylized, Petrarchist mode, sung of his love for Cassandra, Diane's aunt. In his fifth sonnet d'Aubigné recalls the inimitable greatness of the "Prince of Poets":

> Je ne veux à l'envy, pour sa niepce entreprendre
> D'en rechanter autant comme tu as chanté,
> Mais je veux comparer à beauté la beauté,
> Et mes feux à tes feux, et ma cendre à ta cendre.

It is not to copy you that I want to undertake for her niece to write as much poetry as you did, but I want to compare one beauty with another, my love with your love, and my ashes with your ashes.

Nor must we overlook the revival of the mode of Petrarchist images in poetry in the early 1570s in France, for it was a period when Ronsard was composing his *Sonnets pour Hélène* and Desportes the *Amours de Diane,* both collections mirroring court taste.

In the *Hécatombe* we find a large number of themes which occur in other contemporary authors, but d'Aubigné succeeds in the majority of cases in taking these themes and adapting them to suit his own tempestuous temperament. Although his basic idea may come straight from another poet, he often expresses it in an individual manner, drawing upon his rich experience. Herein lies his originality and the secret of his apparent sincerity.

IV *The Personal and the Conventional*

For one critic, the sonnets reflect three phases in the two-year love cycle; hope, doubt, and despair.[6] It is true that a number of sonnets appear to refer to definite events. The poet remembers with ecstasy a moment of tenderness in a shady grove: "O sejour amiable! ô repos pretieux!/O giron, doux support au chef qui se tourmente!" (*PR,* 19) ("Oh friendly sojourn! Oh precious place of rest! Oh lap, a sweet support for a tormented head"); an incident with Diane's coach (*PR,* 30); the trees engraved with their intertwined initials which he planted in the grounds at Talcy (*PR,* 31); Diane's request for "quelque nouveauté" from Paris (*PR,* 36); the reading of his poems (*PR,* 40); the separation from his beloved (*PR,* 48–53); a hard, harsh reply from Diane to the poet which provoked him to cry: "Ha! dame, qui n'es moins stupide qu'orgueilleuse" (*PR*, 69); the day in 1571 when they met: "Et au poinct proprement du solstice..." (*PR*, 86); and her hostility toward him (*PR*, 89).

Throughout the collection, poems blazon forth the celestial beauty of Diane. She is "un chasteau basti de diamans" (*PR*, 17); she has an "oeil imperieux," a "celeste face" (*PR*, 18); her beauty defies the painter's brush (*PR*, 22), for "ces coquins n'ont crayon à vos couleurs pareil" (*PR*, 24, 25). Like so many Petrarchist belles she has golden hair (*PR*, 27), coral lips (*PR*, 28), a graceful ear (*PR*, 33), attractive hands (*PR*, 35), enchanting eyes (*PR*, 37), and a brilliant milky complexion (*PR*, 41) — "le laict est bazané auprès de ce beau teinct" (*PR*, 42), a charming voice and she is an accomplished spinet player:

> Que voy-je? une blancheur à qui la neige est noire,
> Des yeux ravis en soy, de soy mesme esblouis,
> Des oeillets à l'envy, des lys espanouis,
> Des doigts qui prennent lustre à ces marches d'hyvoire.
> (*PR*, 44).

What do I see? a whiteness up against which snow is black, eyes enraptured in themselves, dazzled by themselves, carnations are emulated and flowering lilies, fingers which take luster from these ivory keys.

These praises find their ironic contrary in a sort of anti-*Blason* (*PR*, 68), where the poet laments Diane's hardness of heart: "Je graveray mon nom sur ce coeur endurcy,/Le bruslant de mes feux, le mynant de mes larmes" (*PR*, 68) ("I shall engrave my name on that hardened heart, burning it with the fire of my love, wearing it away with my tears.") Such poems do little to enhance d'Aubigné's reputation or to show him as little more than a fashionable rhymester. The very banality of the imagery gives an impression of *déjà vu* and recalls the *Blason* fashion launched by Clément Marot in the first half of the century.[7]

By naming but a few of the other themes treated by the poet, we can see how conventional his choice has been. Love has triumphed over reason, for "L'amour surmonte tout, qui luy resisteroit?" (*PR*, 13); he is consumed by the fire of love, "De toutes parts je brusle peu à peu..." (*PR*, 26); to be in love is synonymous with death "...je trouve en sa beauté la mort" (*PR*, 99); his beloved is immortal, "Rien n'est mortel en toy" (*PR*, 6); and her eyes have been the vehicle of Cupid's arrows, "Tes yeux en sont les arcs, et tes regards les flesches (*PR,* 100). And yet through his particular handling of such themes the poet raises his collection up from the nadir of mediocrity.

V *The Originality of the Poet*

The poet's originality is to be seen on the two levels of the form and the content of the poems.[8] Drawing on his own experiences, d'Aubigné provides personal extensions to what is frequently a trite Petrarchist conceit. The Wars of Religion furnished him with a fiery stock of epithets, and he felt forced to crave Diane's indulgence, should he appear uncouth by using them:

> Pardonne moy, chere maistresse,
> Si mes vers sentent la destresse,
> Le soldat, la peine et l'esmoy.
> Car depuis qu'en aimant je souffre,
> Il faut qu'ils sentent comme moy
> La poudre, la mesche et le souffre.
>
> (*PR,* 4).

Forgive me, dear mistress, if my lines smack of distress, the soldier, hardship, and agitation. For since I suffer in love they must smack like me of powder, fuses, and sulphur.

The spiritual battle of the senses which love engenders is represented in a materialistic, realistic manner, with reference to real battles and real blood (see *PR,* 7-16). The imagery becomes more vivid by the interplay of the violent imagination of the author, who passes from the simile to a direct confrontation — his tormented, lovesick body becomes the blood-stained battlefield: "Je suis le champ sanglant où la fureur hostile/Vomit le meurtre rouge..." (*PR,* 8) ("I am the blood-stained field where the hostile fury vomits bloody murder..."); and the civil war has been transposed from without to within: "Le debat de mes sens, mon courage inutile.../Qui font de ma raison une guerre civile" (*PR,* 9) ("The debate of my senses, my useless courage... which wage civil war with my mind..."). His fascination for the sight of blood and gory horror is repeated when he compares himself with a soldier lying mortally wounded on the battlefield: "Avecq' le sang, l'ame rouge ravie/Se debattoit dans le sein transpercé" (*PR,* 14) ("Amid the blood, the enraptured red soul struggled within the pierced breast"); and on several occasions he makes an analogy between the winning of Diane and the besieging of a town (*PR,* 15, 16, 94). Although such military terms of comparison are the ones most often quoted by d'Aubigné's critics, they are relatively infrequent. Those we have mentioned, however, reveal an aspect of the author's technique, the use of tangible experience to express abstractions, the desire to arouse interest and attention by the sheer force of the image and by the identification of the poet with the material object. This movement is also to be noticed in the opening sonnets (*PR,* 1-3) which develop the theme of the tempestuous storm at sea, reflecting the precarious state of the poet's soul. He is like a man who has been shipwrecked: "La mer me fait perir pour s'enfler de mes larmes" (*PR,* 1); he is guided on the sea of misfortune by the light of his beloved's eyes: "J'ay veu l'astre beçon des yeux de ma deesse" (*PR,* 2).

Throughout the collection there is a very real presence of death: the relationship between love and death is latent in virtually all contemporary love poetry, but it is rarely given the forcefulness of d'Aubigné's expression and description. By his use of nature themes d'Aubigné panders to contemporary taste, and they will be further developed in the *Stances.* Nature provides the setting for a meeting with Diane (*PR,* 19), an allegory of the Garden of Love (*PR,* 20, 55); the violence of his temperament emerges in a vituperation against Nature:

> Je despite à ce coup ton inique puissance,
> O nature cruelle à tes propres enfantz!
> Terre yvre de mon sang, ô astres rougissantz,
> Bourreaux du ciel injuste, avecq' leur influence.
>
> (*PR,* 60)

I rage at this blow against your iniquitous power, Oh nature who are so cruel toward your own children! Oh earth drunk with my blood, Oh blushing stars, executioners of the unjust heavens, with their influence.

D'Aubigné sees himself as being the microcosm of creation (*PR,* 80, 81): "Cest astre, qui me luit des rayons de son oeil/Fait en moy ce que fait au monde le soleil" (*PR,* 81) ("This star which shines on me with the rays of her eye, does to me what the sun does to the

Le Printemps

world.'') In three sonnets (*PR*, 83-85), he traces the correlation between his love and the seasons, achieving a synthesis of the banal theme and his own idiosyncratic style. For example, sonnet 84 begins:

> Ores qu'on voit le ciel en cent mille bouchons
> Cracheter sur la terre une blanche dragée,
> Et que du gris hyver la perruque chargée
> Enfarine les champs de neige et de glaçons....

Now that we see the heavens in a hundred thousand clouds expectorate on the earth a white sweetmeat, and that the laden locks of grey winter powder the fields with snow and icicles....

Here the force of *cracheter, bouchons, dragée, perruque,* and *enfariner* stresses the materialism of d'Aubigné's language and poetic vision. *Enfariner* was the term used to describe the putting on of an actor's make-up and thus here suggests a masking of the countryside. Toward the end of the sixteenth century this theme of the mask was particularly widespread.[9] It assumes a great importance in the whole of d'Aubigné's poetic output as well as in the *Hécatombe*. The poet is indignant because Diane wears a mask: "Pourquoy me caches-tu le ciel de ton visage/De ce traistre satin, larron de tes beautez?" (*PR*, 34) ("Why do you hide from me the heaven of your face with this treacherous piece of satin, the thief of your beauteous charm?"). He attacks those who falsify their feelings (*PR*, 54), their religion (*PR*, 74), and even turns his venom against the hypocrisy of Diane herself: "Soubz un humble maintien, soubz une douce face,/Tu cache un faux regard, un esclair de menace" (*PR*, 78) ("Behind a demure countenance, a sweet face, you hide a false look, a threatening gleam..."). This innate antipathy for hypocrisy is an essential element of his style. He avoids the coy and honeyed tone of much amatory verse. His lines convey the impression of the sincerity of a man who has had experience of life, who is not the immature "amoureux transi" but a person who has known all the rigors and pains of unrequited love and disappointment. His language is "precious" without being too "recherché," and his constructions, although not always clear (a constant fault in d'Aubigné's poetry), are not pedantic. His use of mythology is restrained and more a reflection of the current poetic trends than of his Protestant background. The meter is varied, and he uses the alexandrine, the heptasyllabic, the octosyllabic, and the decasyllabic lines with equal dexterity. In some ways the decasyllabics, with their elegiac, muted tone, seem to be versions in a different key of sonnets in alexandrines (see *PR,* 14, 26, 37, etc.). The octosyllabic is generally reserved for the *blason* — the descriptive poem with a lyrical bent (see *PR,* 27, 41, 46, etc.), and the only heptasyllabic poem is of a strongly epigrammatic inspiration (*PR,* 91). He does not possess the *style doux-coulant* of a Desportes, and the rhythm often reflects the violence of his passion. This is well illustrated in sonnet 12:

> Souhaitte qui voudra la mort inopinée
> D'un plomb meurtrier et prompt au hazard envoyé,
> D'un coutelas bouchier, d'un boulet foudroyé,
> Crever poudreux, sanglant, au champ d'une journée.
>
> Souhaitte qui voudra une mort entournée
> De medecins, de pleurs, et un lit coutoyé
> D'heritiers, de criards, puis estre convoyé
> De cent torches en feu à la fosse ordonnée.
>
> Je ne veux pour le solde estre au champ terrassé,
> On en est aujourd'huy trop mal recompensé;
> Je trouve l'autre mort longue, bigotte et folle.
>
> Quoy donc? brusler d'amour que Diane en douleurs
> Serre ma triste cendre infuse dans ses pleurs,
> Puis au sein d'Artemise un tombeau de Mausole.

Let him who wishes desire unforeseen death from a murderous and swift chance shot, from a butchering cutlass, from being struck down by a bullet, from dying stained with dust and blood on the field after a day's battle.

Let him who wishes, desire a death surrounded by doctors and tears, and his bed bordered by his heirs and weeping persons, and then accompanied by a hundred flaming torches to the appointed grave.

I do not want as payment to be struck to the ground, today we are too badly rewarded, and I find the other death, long, hypocritical, and mad.

What then? to burn and love so that Diane in sadness will gather up my ashes mixed with her tears, then to be within Artemis's bosom in a mausoleum.

The theme had been treated, *inter alios,* by Ovid and Desportes, but neither gave their renderings the force of d'Aubigné's. The abruptness of the first line with its imperative subjunctive, the

Le Printemps

"de" in the quatrains and the "je" in the first tercet, the succession of adjectives and adjectival phrases, the use of enjambment and syncopation, help to break up the flow of the poem and add to the general feeling of disdain experienced by the poet for these forms of death. D'Aubigné has sought out the telling epithet with his felicitous use of *inopinée, meurtrier, bouchier, poudreux, sanglant*. The enjambment and calm of the final tercet contrast with the staccato rhythm and strident imagery which precede. The introduction of the classical image in the last line adds a powerful poetic dimension. That the poet was anxious to achieve the maximum evocative effect is evident when we compare the last four lines of the sonnet with those which appear in an earlier version:

> Je trouve l'autre mort bigotte et dure
> Mais tué par tes mains, mourir entre tes bras
> Avoir tes yeux pour plombs, et pour le coutelas
> Mille soupirs tranchans, ton coeur pour sepulture.

I find the other death both hypocritical and hard, but [I should like to be] killed by your hands, to die in your arms, to have your eyes for shot, and for a cutlass a thousand piercing sighs, your heart for my tomb.

This contains the same basic sentiments as the final poem but expresses them somewhat prosaically.[10] Nor should we overlook the artistry of the sound and structure of line 1; in addition, in line 2, *prompt* echoes *plomb*, in line 3, *coutelas bouchier* is mirrored in *boulet foudroyé*, and in line 4, *sanglant* in *champ*, *poudreux* in *journée*; while lines 6 and 7 have the same metrical structure, and in line 8, *torches* announces *ordonnée* and *feu, fosse*. Such stylistic features reveal the care with which d'Aubigné composed his verse. Not all the sonnets are as successful as the one quoted; not always is the content treated in a way worthy of a great poet; but, nonetheless, the collection provides an interesting introduction to one of the facets of d'Aubigné's manifold creative personality and of an age which has often been called, though not without reservations, baroque.

VI *The Influence of Nérac*

To be added to the sonnets of the *Hécatombe* are twenty-two *Stances* and fifty-one *Odes*.[11] These are not all dedicated to Diane but seem to have formed in d'Aubigné's mind part of *Le Printemps*. Mademoiselle Droz has studied one of the major manuscripts of these two works, the Monmerqué manuscript,[12] and believes that it is the *Album de vers* belonging to Marguerite de Valois, queen of Navarre. It contains, amongst other things, twenty-one of the *Stances* and thirty-four of the *Odes*. It is known that d'Aubigné spent some time at Nérac and it is estimated that only nine of the *Stances* were written actually for Diane, the other poems having been composed for the ladies-in-waiting at the court and even for Marguerite de Valois herself. The poet omitted a number of *Odes* from the manuscript, because when it was compiled Marguerite had, since 1585, been a partisan of the Catholic League and hence was considered an enemy by the Protestants. Also, by that time d'Aubigné was probably ashamed of his poet-courtier relationship. Thus in a list of the *incipit* drawn up in the author's own hand and figuring in manuscript 159, fourteen *Stances* and twenty-one *Odes* are missing.

During his stay at Nérac the poet seems to have led a life of gay abandon and to have formed part of a group of pleasure seekers known as the *Doemogorgonistes,* even going so far perhaps as to write ribald songs for his friends (see *Ode, 47*).[13] He also spent some time at Henry's court at Pau for he later recalls, in a letter to the king's sister Catherine, how she used to sing his *Odes* "comme liant d'or et de soye ces fleurs de printemps."[14] In view of the fact that the inspiration of many of the *Odes* was so varied and profane, it is not surprising that in later years the poet felt guilty about their subject matter and did not try to have his youthful poetic efforts published.

By composing *Stances* and *Odes,* d'Aubigné was following, yet again, a contemporary fashion. Others, be it Hesteau de Nuysement, Boyssières, La Meschinière, or La Jessée, also practiced these genres, but it is to Philippe Desportes that must be attributed the credit for their popularity in the 1570s. Although Ronsard had effectively launched the ode, it was Desportes who had developed their use, and before d'Aubigné had made the metrical distinction between alexandrines for the *Stances* and octosyllabics and a shorter meter for the *Odes*.[15]

VII   *The* Stances

After the comparatively compact nature of the sonnets, the

reader is surprised by his sudden confrontation with the open-ended form of the *Stances*.[16] They vary enormously in length — from 16 lines (*PR*, 2) to 304 (*PR*, 20). We can sense the dynamic personality of their author and the atmosphere of the Navarre courts in their tone and expression. The poet gives vent to his feelings with a fury which has its origins more in his own passionate nature than in the inspiration of Apollo.[17] The *Stances* display a multitude of themes and variations of mood, some of which establish a link with the *Hécatombe* — the separation of the heart and the body (*PR*, 2); the indifference of the beloved in the face of the poet's suffering (*PR*, 6); the parallel between physical and spiritual torment (*PR*, 7); the Petrarchist beauty of the loved one (*PR*, 10); the poet's dislike of insincerity (*PR*, 15). Other poems introduce new topics, not always connected with his passion for Diane: the ecstasy of a kiss from a mistress, "Ma bouch' oza toucher la bouche cramoysie/Pour coeuillir, sans la mort, l'immortelle beaulté" (*PR*, 13) ("My mouth dared touch the crimson mouth to gather, without death, the immortal beauty"); an exposition of the origin of love according to Plato (*PR*, 17); and a number of *Stances* are addressed to Olympe, encouraging her to love in her widowhood (*PR*, 18). Were all these poems written as an expression of d'Aubigné's own feelings? Let it suffice to recall the apparent sincerity and beauty of Ronsard's collection of sonnets *Sur la mort de Marie* which contains many poems written for Henri III on the death of his love, Marie de Clèves. Similarly, in these *Stances* and *Odes* composed for others we see the influence of Platonic conceptions of love and Petrarchan conceits, interest in which was prevalent in Marguerite de Valois's entourage.[18] Henri Weber's edition of the *Stances* illustrates fully the popularity of the themes exploited by d'Aubigné; yet, if we compare his efforts with those of his contemporaries and of his predecessors, he stands out by the sheer violence of expression. The reader is constantly startled by the repetition of the images of blood, death, and water, the recurring macabre atmosphere, the clear-cut dualism which d'Aubigné confers upon his imaginative world. The poet's love of antithesis and emphatic contrast, a constant feature of *Les Tragiques*, is already noticeable, as is the opposition of good and evil, God and Man. At times the mere addition of a macabre note raises the poem up from the platitudinous and the mediocre. After a succession of precious images in an appeal to Olympe (*PR*, 18), the poet introduces the last stanza thus:

> Je suis l'Ethna bruslant en ma flamme profonde,
> Tu es le Nil heureux qui espanche ton unde
> Sur la terre qui meurt de la soif de tes eaux;
> Noie les feuz, mignonne, embrazeurs de mon ame,
> Ou me laisse brusler ton Nil dedans ma flamme,
> Que je noye en tes pleurs, ou seche en mes flambeaux.

I am Etna burning within my deep flame, you are the blessed Nile which spills its waves over the earth dying from thirst of your waters; drown the flames, Oh sweet one, which set my soul on fire, or let me burn your Nile within my flame, let me drown in your tears, or dry [them] with the fire of my passion.

His descriptions of nature have a plastic reality underlining his fertile imagination and his possession of a mind prone to visions and melancholia. In the first of the *Stances* he expands the theme of the lover in despair who vainly seeks consolation in the wilderness of nature. François d'Amboise had already imitated the Italian forerunners of these *disperata* in 1571, but d'Aubigné in his poem pushes the description of the macabre to its literary extreme. The poet describes the hermit's retreat in terms worthy of the ascetism of the monks of the Counter-Reformation: "Le lieu de mon repos est une chambre peinte/De mil os blanchissans et de testes de mortz" ("The place of my rest is a room painted with a thousand whitening bones and skulls"). As Floyd Gray has pointed out[19] there were two conceptions of melancholy prevalent in the sixteenth century: one was the Aristotelian view describing melancholy as a condition which endowed its sufferers with intellectual acumen, profundity, artistic ability, etc. (see Ronsard and Petrarch), the other was the Galenic comment that melancholy was a degrading mental abnormality associated with fear and sorrow. It produced either "sottish lethargy or insanity accompanied by sorrowful and fearful delusion." It is the latter conception that d'Aubigné appears to have espoused, for he placed the *Stances* under the sign of sad Saturn, the planet associated with melancholy:

> Que du blond Apollon le rayon doré n'entre
> En ma grotte sans jour, que jamais de son euil
> Nul planete ne jette un rayon dans mon antre,
> Sinon Saturne seul pour incliner au deuil.

(*PR*, 1)

Le Printemps

May the gilded rays of the fair Apollo never enter into my lightless cave, may no planet with its eye ever cast a ray into my lair, unless it be Saturn alone to provoke mourning.

As a symbol of the difficulties of winning the love of an important woman, the poet evokes the ascent of a mountain. The woman in question may well have been Marguerite (her attributes were the sun and an eye),[20] and the mountains the Pyrenees. He gives the precious image of the final stage of the climb:

> Je monte, je rencontre après
> Du chault soleil la vive face
> Qui devant moy faict fondre exprès
> Les amas de neige et de glace.
> Soleilz d'amour, fondés aussy
> De ma beauté la froide grace
> Qui, comme neige et comme glace,
> Est blanche et froide tout ainsy.
>
> (*PR*, 20)

I climb up, then I meet the lively face of the warm sun which on purpose, causes the heaps of snow and ice to melt before me. Suns of love, melt also the cool charm of my beauteous one who, like snow and ice is just as white and cold.

This passage contrasts with the violence of his emotions during the ascent, which can be compared with the violence of a mountain stream:

> Que veullent ces torrens, ces eaux,
> Filles des neiges, des oraiges,
> Sy la raige de ses ruisseaux
> Ne bruit aussi fort que mes raiges?
> L'aveugle fureur de ses ours
> Ces monstres veullent-ilz abatre
> Celuy qui a pour les combattre
> Les feux et les fers des amours?
>
> (*PR*, 20)

What do these torrents, these waters, daughters of the snow and the storms mean, if the rage of its streams does not resound as loudly as does my rage? What is the meaning of the blind fury of its bears, do these monsters want to kill him who has the fire and irons of love to fight them with?

Elsewhere the poet seeks pity through a horrific exposition of his suffering:

> J'ouvre mon estommac, une tumbe sanglante
> De maux enseveliz: pour Dieu, tourne tes yeux,
> Diane, et voy au fond mon cueur party en deux
> Et mes poumons gravez d'une ardeur viollente....
>
> *(PR, 6)*

I open up my bosom, a bloody tomb of hidden troubles: in God's name, turn your gaze, Diane, and look in the depths at my heart split in two and my lungs marked by violent passion....

Antithesis and paradox are used to create the impression of mental anguish:

> Ha! cors vollé du cueur, tu brusle sans ta flamme,
> Sans esprit je respire et mon pis et mon mieux,
> J'affecte sans vouloir, je m'anyme sans ame,
> Je vis sans avoir sang, je regarde sans yeux.
>
> *(PR, 2)*

Ah! Oh body bereft of your heart, you are burning without a flame, without life I breathe in what is good and bad for me, I have desires without wishing, I move without a soul, I live without any blood, I look without eyes.

By means of such devices, d'Aubigné succeeds in arousing our sympathy and in creating a dramatic and dynamic effect — this impression of dynamism is enhanced by the very use of the strophic form. The rhythm is varied, the alexandrine being the most popular meter. The abrupt syntax, the end-stopping of the stanzas without a smooth liaison, all help to evoke the picture of a passionate poet living in a disordered world. Whether the blood and war images are due to his personal experience or to literary convention is a moot point, but it is the general effect which is important. The degree of success is not the same in every poem, and the *Stances* which stand out are numbers 1-9, 13, 19, 20; for it is in these that d'Aubigné manages to capture the movement and the quintessence of passion in an individualistic and powerful manner, thereby telling us much about himself and the literary tastes of his age.

VIII *The* Odes

The unifying factor of this varied collection of poems is their lyricism. Many of them would fit musical settings and could well have been sung at the Béarnais courts. Their inspiration varies from the sublime to the grotesque. A number represent continuations of themes already hinted at in the previous two parts, and develop the general line of poems written in honor of Diane (see *Odes* 1–8). The lyrical qualities of the Ronsardian ode are recaptured at times by the younger poet, as in *Ode* 8:

> Soubs la tremblante courtine
> De ses bessons arbrisseaux,
> Au murmure qui chemine
> Dans ses gasouillans ruisseaux,
> Sur un chevet touffu esmaillé des coulleurs
> D'un million de fleurs.[21]

Beneath the quivering curtain of its twin bushes, to the murmuring sound which meanders through its babbling streams, on a tufted seat all bright with the colors of a million flowers....

However, d'Aubigné is often content just to Petrarchize, no doubt in order to curry favor at court, and such efforts are similar to those of a whole host of other court poets of the 1570s and 1580s. Some odes have obviously been penned with a circumstantial purpose in mind, such as the epithalamium (*PR*, 15) or the ode for Antoine-Mathieu de Laval (*PR*, 39). Mademoiselle Droz suggests that odes 36 and 37 with their inherent "pauses" were the libretti for a court ballet. Their theme of Platonic love would certainly support such a hypothesis. Other odes reveal that precious style which rings with such hollowness through court poetry at the end of the sixteenth century, for example,

> Des dars qui partent de tes yeux,
> De leur belle flamme divine
> Il m'a transpercé la poictrine
> Et bruslé le cueur amoureux:
> Mais si tu me praiste faveur,
> Le vaincu sera le vaincqueur.

(*PR*, 43)

With arrows which shoot from your eyes, with their beautiful divine flame, he has pierced my bosom and burnt my heart in love, but if you grant me your favor the conquered will be conqueror.

A curiosity is found in the rhymed dialogues between Diane and d'Aubigné (*PR,* 44, 45), and the poet's body and soul (*PR,* 46): a form which is also used by Ronsard in the *Sonnets pour Hélène.* At times d'Aubigné's youthful, soldierly mood emerges with a touch of the *esprit gaulois,* and he continues the tradition of Ronsard as seen in his *Livret de folastries* (1553) when he indulges in those invective poems so popular with members of a closed society. We find the theme of the young beauty chaperoned by an old hag (*PR,* 23) which is reminiscent of Joachim Du Bellay's *Antérotique de la jeune et de la vieille amie;* and the same author's *Contre une vieille*[22] is at the source of *Ode 23.* The description of the old woman is worthy of the personification of the vices to be found in *La Chambre dorée:*

> L'autre a la perruque taigneuse
> D'une acquenée farcyneuse,
> Un combat dessus et dessoubz
> De punaises avecq' les pous:
> Tout grouille et tout cela s'assemble,
> Et tout ce gros amas resemble
> Au poil d'un vieux barbet croté,
> Au fruit d'un serpent avorté.

The other has the moth-ridden old wig of a glanders-ridden hag, a fight above and below between bugs and lice: all is acrawl and all that meets, and all this great heap looks like the hair on the face of a dirty old spaniel, or like a serpent's abortive fruit.

His attacks against a "slanderess" (*PR,* 24) and the old prostitute Marroquin (*PR,* 25) indicate the currency of a literary tradition which was to continue when Henri became Henri IV, as is so ably illustrated in Régnier's thirteenth *Satire,* "Macette." When such poems are considered alongside the traditional Petrarchist forms of beauty, they provide examples of the parallel development of the antiheroine in verse. Some of the poems are mere bagatelles (see *PR,* 27, 42) pointing to the banality of sophisticated court amusement; *Ode 47,* on the other hand, is more a reflection of the drinking bout and bawdy songs which so often accompany a rout.

Le Printemps 37

All in all, the *Odes* present us with a potpourri of taste and a similar diversity of rhythm. As is to be expected in an essentially lyrical collection, the prosaic, heroic alexandrine is rarely used. When it does occur, it is more often than not in conjunction with hexameters. The majority of the verse is in octo- and heptasyllabics, thus emphasizing the songlike, slight nature of the inspiration.

IX Conclusion

In *Le Printemps* we see how the young d'Aubigné made his poetic début, how his passionate and fiery temperament was clearly detectable right at the outset of his literary career. The collection reveals too the influence of contemporary fashion on the youthful poet — conscious of his debt to Ronsard, he appears to have made a definite attempt in the *Hécatombe* and the *Stances* to follow the current literary conventions but at the same time to adapt them to suit his own particular view of the world. In the *Odes,* where he is more slavishly subservient to the dictates of courtly taste than to his own inclinations, his real personality is less prominent. *Le Printemps* is not without its blemishes: there are many obstacles to the enjoyment of the modern reader — the use of clichés, the preciosity, the repetitiveness, etc. — but, generally speaking, the poems justify the careful effort required to read and understand them, forming as they do an excellent introduction to the poetic works of our author and to the best of Béarnais court poetry. The originality of d'Aubigné lies in his imagery, which brings to his poems a distinctive violence, realism, and thereby a gratifying freshness.[23]

CHAPTER 3

A Poetic Vision — Les Tragiques

SERIOUSLY wounded at the battle of Castel-Jaloux at the end of the fifth War of Religion in June, 1577, d'Aubigné took refuge on his estate of the Landes-Guinemer. The doctors despaired of his life and he himself dictated to a *Juge du lieu*[1] the first lines of *Les Tragiques* which he considered to be his "testament."[2] He probably worked upon the poem during the next two years and was to come back to it in later years to "polish and expand it." There is no doubt that it is for this poem that the author is best known. It is a mammoth work of some seven books, 9302 lines and a preface of 414 lines. It is also a book which caused a stir in the author's own lifetime, enjoying two editions, the first in 1616 (Maillé) and the second in 1623 (Geneva). The work appeared at first anonymously with the letters L.B.D.D., that is, Le Bouc du Désert, which was a penname for d'Aubigné, but the second edition bore the name of the author. From 1577 to 1616 there is a span of thirty-nine years which constitutes a remarkable part of the author's lifetime and covers one of the most troubled epochs in the history of France. Throughout this period, d'Aubigné turned to *Les Tragiques* periodically to make them more up-to-date and more resonant. Garnier[3] considers that of the seven books, the first four, *Misères, Princes, La Chambre dorée,* and *Les Feux,* have their origin in the early period with later additions, as does the sixth book, *Vengeances.* Books five, *Les Fers,* and seven, *Jugement,* would have been started at a later date, probably about the turn of the century.

D'Aubigné was able to draw upon his own experience, and that of his contemporaries, in the Wars of Religion which raged for thirty years from 1562 onward. Coupled with this is his firsthand knowledge of life at court, not only that of Henry III, but also that of Henry de Navarre, later Henry IV, and that of the regency of Louis XIII.

I D'Aubigné's Conception of Les Tragiques

The massacre of the Protestants in Paris and subsequently throughout France on St. Bartholomew's Day, 1572, had made a tremendous impact upon the impressionable d'Aubigné. His own moral fiber, and that of the whole Protestant cause, had been severely affected by this dastardly action. Persecuted throughout the century, the Protestants' morale was at a particularly low ebb in the 1570s when the Wars of Religion were entering their second decade of bloody existence. *Les Tragiques* represent an effort by an ardent and committed Protestant to bring consolation to his religious party and to record for all time in literature the great deeds of the faithful and the extent of their suffering. The aim of *Les Tragiques* was not to give a day-by-day factual account of contemporary events but to produce a work which would have an emotional effect upon the reader:

We are bored by books which instruct, give us ones which will move us, in a century where all Christian zeal is extinguished, where the difference between the real and the lie is all but abolished, where the hands of the enemies of the church hide the blood with which they are stained beneath the presents, and their cruelty beneath the generosity. (*T*, p. 3)

For the historical narration of the Protestant suffering it is necessary to consult the *Histoire universelle,* for the two books form a diptych: on one side there is the factual, impartial prose account and on the other the impassioned vision of a poet. Although d'Aubigné's partisan feelings are evident in the *Histoire,* they are reduced to a minimum; whereas in *Les Tragiques* no holds are barred, and he gives full vent to his feelings. What he captures in his poem is the notion of the injustice and of the suffering meted out to the Protestants, as well as that of hope in the eternal goodness of God, who, although He works in mysterious ways, will reward the faithful in due course. The poet is also attached emotionally to his poetic production; as with Montaigne, his work is *consubstantiel à son auteur.*

There is, as in all d'Aubigné's work, a great emphasis on truth and the spontaneity of its gestation. The book responds to an inner need for the poet to express himself, but one should not overlook, however, the literary ambitions of the work. As can be seen from d'Aubigné's other writings, there is a great variety in the forms he uses. He was influenced considerably by Ronsard and the Pléiade, and it is no small coincidence that the sixteenth-century authors were in search of an epic poem which would do justice to the French language and genius, thereby raising its literature up to a level comparable with that of the ancients. Joachim Du Bellay in *La Deffence et Illustration de la langue françoise* had already, in 1549, exhorted the would-be poet to choose "quelque un de ces beaulx vieulx romans Francoys, comme un Lancelot, un Tristan, ou autres: & en fay renaitre au monde un admirable Iliade et labourieuse Eneïde.... Telle oeuvre certainement seroit à leur immortelle gloire, honneur de la France, et grande illustration de nostre langue." ("one of those fine old French Romances, such as a Lancelot, or a Tristan or others: and to recreate it into an admirable Iliad and a taxing Aeneid.... Such a work would certainly be for their immortal glory, the honor of France and a great illustration of our language.") We know how Ronsard had accepted the challenge but had to admit defeat with his incomplete *La Franciade* which appeared in 1572, only a few years before d'Aubigné started *Les Tragiques*.

In 1562, Ronsard had shown how it was possible to write good poetry on a political and religious theme in his *Discours sur les misères de ce temps*. On the Protestant side, the poets of the last third of the sixteenth century were very often concerned with polemics, religious problems or translations of the Psalms, as is to be seen in the works of Jean de Sponde or Guillaume Du Bartas. It was Du Bartas who, in 1579, published *La Création du monde ou Première Semaine* and in 1584, *La Seconde Semaine*. In this poem the author sought to trace the history of the Christian faith and religion since its origins. D'Aubigné therefore may have seen *Les Tragiques* as a poetic opportunity of contributing to the literary aims of the Pléiade, of endowing France with a work of epic proportions which would serve simultaneously the Protestant cause. It was an honorable method of atoning for the apparent guilt he felt at having composed his earlier collection of poetry, *Le Printemps,* which, although it was not published during his lifetime, was on a profane subject, his love for Diane de Talcy. He refers in derogatory terms to his collection in the preface when he speaks of "Un pire et plus heureux aisné,/Plus beau et moins plein de sagesse" (*T,* ll.56–57) ("A worse and happier elder brother, more beautiful and with less wisdom"); and he returns to this theme in the opening pages of *Misères* where he proclaims:

A Poetic Vision—Les Tragiques

> Je n'escris plus les feux d'un amour inconu,
> Mais, par l'application plus sage devenu,
> J'entreprens bien plus haut, car j'apprens à ma plume
> Un autre feu, auquel la France se consume.
>
> (*T*, ll.55-58)

I write no longer about the fiery passion of an unknown love, but wiser through my diligence, I am undertaking a more noble enterprise, for I am teaching my pen another fire, one which is destroying France.

Such lines suggest that in *Les Tragiques* he was revealing a different, more important sort of love and passion, one which transcends man's mortal nature. D'Aubigné was not alone among the Protestant poets in his denunciation of a youthful literary endeavor. Théodore de Bèze expressed public regret for his *Juvenilia* and stressed in the *Aux lecteurs* of his play, *Abraham sacrifiant* (1550), how he was turning his attention to more serious, religious themes after the love poetry of his younger days.

Prompted by literary ambition, d'Aubigné, although greatly influenced by Pléiade poetics, had a different conception of the way he would undertake the construction of his poem. He did not intend composing a purely fictitious work, one based upon the systematic reconstruction of Greek and Roman myths; for the most part, he turns his back on this source of material. His poem is based upon fact, upon living experience. The poet considers that his poem has been conceived as a result of a privileged insight into the workings of the divinity. He appears to have had, like St Teresa or Ignatius Loyola, a mystical experience. Later we shall see how this visionary quality colors the whole work, and yet it could be interpreted as an example of poetic license, with d'Aubigné substituting for the fury of the Muse-inspired profane poets, the holy fury of the Christian prophet. For like a latter day Jeremiah, the poet sees himself as an interpreter of divine will, even going so far as to incorporate into his poem certain prophecies, or rather "apophéties," as he playfully terms them. These are forecasts of certain events which had already occurred before the publication of the book. Nevertheless, not all the prophecies should be considered as having been added *post factum,* for some, d'Aubigné states, should be looked upon "comme escrites avant les choses advenues" (*T*, p. 7).[4]

Why did d'Aubigné choose his title of *Les Tragiques?* In the *Aux lecteurs* he goes over the styles of the various books, and it is obvious that there exists in his mind a close parallel between what he has written and the prevalent conception of sixteenth-century tragedy. The aim of *Les Tragiques* is to "move," and its subject is that of the troubles that have beset the Protestants — this is all reminiscent of Jean de La Taille's views on tragedy as set out in the preface to his play, *Saül le furieux* (1572), and which are not only illustrated in the construction of his own plays but also in those of Garnier and other contemporaries. For La Taille, true tragedy "... only treats the pitiful ruin of great lords, the uncertainties of fortune, exiles, wars, plagues, famine, captivities, the horrible cruelty of tyrants; in brief, only of tears and extreme sorrow, and not of things which occur every day naturally and for ordinary reasons...." The accent in style is on the "pathétique," on the desire to arouse pity in the hearts of the spectators, "For the subject must be so pitiful and moving in itself that even when it is only resumed or stated briefly, it creates compassion within us." Although there are expectedly great differences between the structure of tragedy and of *Les Tragiques,* there is still a similarity of tone. The title can be seen also to recall the visionary nature of d'Aubigné's conception, for, as he remarks in *Misères,* "Voyez la tragedie, abbaissez vos courages,/Vous n'estes spectateurs, vous estes personnages" (*T,* I, ll.169–70) ("Look at the tragedy, humble yourselves, you are not spectators, you are actors").

The words "tragédie" and "tragique" appear with amazing frequency throughout the text, and in *Misères* he invokes Melpomene, the muse of tragedy (*T,* I, 1.79). In the elaboration of his scenario he reveals his religious conception of the world. Mortal man and his often sinful ways are opposed to the ever bountiful and generous wisdom of the eternal God. D'Aubigné, with that forceful nature of his, reaffirms his belief in the Protestant faith, interpreting the events of Christian history in the light of his biblical knowledge and religious convictions. Such a commentary on historical happenings with its single-mindedness of intent and illustration enables the reader, in the words of Professor McFarlane, "to sense the unity of Being behind the vicissitudes of Time."[5] The Bible for d'Aubigné is the only document which can provide the key to divine truth. Its teaching permeates the whole of the poem, as does that of Calvin with his belief that God will reward the faithful and punish their wicked persecutors in the afterlife.

A Poetic Vision—Les Tragiques

Let it not be forgotten, however, that d'Aubigné is not merely a propagandist or a polemicist; he is also a poet. This is evident from his attitude toward classical mythology, as it is revealed in a curious document addressed to his children, *L'Hercule chrétien*.[6] In this work he warns them about the fallacious nature of ancient myths, for they were produced by the ignorance of men of antiquity of the true God; and yet, the myths can be taken as moral examples which fit well into the Christian ethic. Here he is following the thought of the enlightened humanists of whom perhaps Erasmus was the most outstanding example. Taking the case of Hercules, the author singles out twelve labors which can be interpreted in a Christian sense, thus showing the allegorical nature of d'Aubigné's view of historical literature. For him Hercules represents the struggle between good and evil, virtue and vice — the episode of the Erymanthean boar is, he declares, full of instruction for his contemporaries since:

Il faut vaincre en nous-mesmes la nature porcine, qui nous fait gaster les beautez que nature nous concedoit, nous rend porceaux en paresse, en gourmandise et en appetis sauvages, et nous fait tousjours retourner en la boüe et au souil de nos ordures. Cette là est la victoire la plus necessaire à l'Hercule Chrestien."

We have to overcome the piglike nature within us, which makes us spoil the beauties that Nature gave us, turns us into pigs by idleness, gluttony, and wild desires, and makes us return always to the mud and mire of our filth. This is the victory which is the most necessary for the Christian Hercules.

Similarly, as Hercules struggled to save and protect Hesione, so the Christian should strive toward freeing the church "enchaisnee sous la Tyrannie du grand monstre des eaux, et de la beste qui la poursuit jusques dans le désert" (in chains beneath the tyranny of the great monster of the waters, and of the beast which pursues it into the desert).

This poetic disposition on the author's part to take everything as being of moral value gives support to the view of history, in that, *plus ça change, plus c'est la même chose.*

II Content and Structure

Les Tragiques comprises seven books, seven no doubt because of the religious and mystic symbolism attached to that number. The books are of varying length, extending from the 1062 lines of *La Chambre dorée* to the 1564 lines of the fifth book, *Les Fers*.

Using a literary technique to be exploited later in the fictional literature of the eighteenth century, d'Aubigné introduces the poem with an *Aux lecteurs* which, although in effect by his own hand, purports to have been composed by the editor who, like Prometheus, has stolen the manuscript from his master: hence the description on the title page of *Les Tragiques,* "donnez au public par le larcin de Promethee" (1616). The *Avis* expounds the author's aims in composing the work: it is to move the reader; it is his testament to posterity, recording tales of valor which would have been suppressed by false historians. The so-called editor bemoans the fact that the manuscript is so untidy, with crossings out and gaps — a personal reflection upon the tempestuous nature of the author. It is of note that the editor's surmise that the author would include probably a commentary on the more erudite allusions in the text in a second edition was never substantiated. The editor claims three reasons have prompted him to publish the work; his love of the church, the author's honor which is at stake because of the indiscriminate borrowings from the manuscript prior to its publication, and the gratitude to be gained from the leading people of his century. The question of the author's style is touched upon, the editor stressing d'Aubigné's unwillingness to read through the text once it had been written. This point was probably added to forestall any eventual criticism, as in the following remark about the use of "quelques mots qui sentent le vulgaire," which is supported by a quotation from one of Ronsard's theoretical works, and the next about the use of rhymes. Such a statement could also be seen as an indication of d'Aubigné's sense of spontaneous inspiration as he composed, one which it would have been improper to rearrange.

In the general description of the style of the seven books, *Misères* is a "tableau piteux du Royaume en general, d'un style bas et tragique, n'excedant que fort peu les loix de la narration"; *Princes* is "d'un style moyen mais satyrique" as is *La Chambre dorée; Les Feux* is "tout entier au sentiment de la religion de l'autheur et d'un style tragicque moyen," whereas *Les Fers* is "du style tragicque eslevé, plus poëtic et plus hardi que les autres": the description given of *Vengeances* is "theologien et historial," and of the final book, *Jugement,* "d'un style eslevé, tragicque." The Greek title

Ubris for the third book and *Dan,* of Latin origin, for the seventh were abandoned in favor of the French names. The editor mentions other works of d'Aubigné which were still in unpublished form, among them being the *Histoire universelle,* which, he claims, shows astonishing impartiality on the part of its author. The *Avis* serves in its closing pages to answer the accusation made against d'Aubigné that he was more in favor of an aristocratic government than a monarchic system as the best for the French and that he has never written against kings but only against tyrants, for as he states in some stanzas quoted from his *Discours par Stances:*

> Le Roi regnant par soi, aussi humble que brave,
> Est l'image de Dieu; mais du tyran esclave
> Le dur gouvernement image de l'Enfer.

The King who reigns on his own, as humble as he is courageous, is the image of God; but the hard rule of an enslaved tyrant is the image of Hell.

All in all, the *Avis* is a carefully worded presentation of the poem, for it takes into account the poet's aims as well as revealing his connection with contemporary poets and his attitude toward his own work. The author's modesty may also be associated with the traditional tone of sixteenth-century *avant-propos.*

The preface, with its octosyllabic line, and the familiarity which is established between the author and his book, recaptures the engaging tone of a Ronsard or of a Montaigne. Obviously composed just before the publication of the poem, it shows the author's premonitions about his impending exile. He opens on the theme of "être" and "paraître" with a reference to the book's unostentatious exterior but rich content. D'Aubigné repeats his insistence upon the close relationship between his book and truth in a very stylized biblical manner. The allusions to the biblical symbolism of the church are not always easy for a modern reader to grasp, but he uses them to emphasize the eternity of the church's message and also to show how, because of his mystical experience, he is in a privileged position to judge the "beaux combats de l'Eglise." He looks ahead to the final book and to the reward of the faithful in heaven. God works on us through our hearts and chooses the strongest to combat tyrants; but when the church is full of the fainthearted, "Alors Dieu affoiblit sa force,/La maudit et tous ses moyens" (*T,* preface, ll.269-70) ("Then God weakens its strength, curses it and all its means"). With hindsight he reflects on the fortune of the Protestants to have had such a prince as Henry de Navarre, but he also pretends to take a step back in time so as to be able to prophesy that the future Henry IV will be assassinated if he goes against God:

> Quand ta bouche renoncera
> Ton Dieu, ton Dieu la percera,
> Punissant le membre coulpable;
> Quand ton coeur, desloyal mocqueur,
> Comme elle sera punissable,
> Alors Dieu percera ton coeur.
> (*T,* preface, ll.325-30)

When your mouth renounces your God, your God will pierce it, punishing the guilty part; when your heart, unfaithful mocker, will be punishable like your mouth, then God will pierce your heart.

Such an "apophétie" was based upon the attempt against Henry IV's life by the Jesuit Châtel, in December, 1594, when the king was wounded in the lips, and upon the king's eventual murder by Ravaillac on May 14, 1610.

Truth is not to be found in the court, exclaims the poet, thus heralding his onslaught on court life in *Princes,* and later in the *Avantures du Baron de Faeneste.* He forestalls the critics of his task by maintaining that he is attacking "les Dieux de la terre," and that his aim is not to flatter those who are satirized in his verse. The faithful and the wicked will find contrary meanings in what he has to say: "Vous louerez Dieu, ils trembleront;/Vous chanterez, ils pleureront" (*T,* preface, ll.373-74) ("You will praise God, they will tremble, you will sing and they will cry"). The preface ends with a simulation of fatigue from the effect of the fury of his inspiration, a theme which recalls the closing pages of Pontus de Tyard's *Solitaire premier,* and finally the poet dedicates his poetic creation to the service of God, the church, Justice, and Truth.

The seven books of the poem follow a set pattern as regards the exposition and view of time. *Misères* describes the present state of France, the misery and the suffering of the French people, and blames the rulers for the misfortunes which have befallen them. In *Princes,* the royal family and their entourage of courtiers are taken

A Poetic Vision—Les Tragiques

to task in no uncertain terms for their behavior. The satirical sword is no less sharp in *La Chambre dorée,* where it is directed at the corruption of the law courts. Against this background of vice, injustice, and oppression, we are introduced in *Les Feux* to a survey of those who have died courageously in the face of inhuman adversity as martyrs to their faith. Such conditions and cruelty have provoked the military action described in *Les Fers,* which has, as its centerpiece, the St. Bartholomew's Day Massacre. From the contemporary scene, d'Aubigné then whisks the reader/spectator/actor away to study the historical precedents, and develops at length the punishment that God has meted out to those who have gone against him. In *Vengeances* d'Aubigné goes back to the primeval murder of Abel by Cain, which he deems to be the start of the opposition between the faithful and the profane seekers after power. The ensuing immense historical survey brings us back once more to the present, and finally in *Jugement* we are transported into a vision of the future, of the Day of Judgment when "the trumpet shall sound, and the dead shall be raised incorruptible, and we shall be changed." At that time the true rewards and punishments will be meted out, and the eventual fate of the faithful will be seen to justify the sufferings that have been described in the early books.

By adopting such a time scheme d'Aubigné has taken a global and finite view of humanity in divine terms. He has raised himself above the confusing morass of contemporary events, of moral corruption and criminal action, in order to replace the present in the history of mankind, and to allow the faithful to transcend their miserable mortal existence and savor the spiritual joys to come, to see where they figure in God's plans for the world. For the faithful it is a message which takes them from present anguish to future bliss; for their oppressors it is one of atonement for temporary pleasure through the awful and horrific sufferings of eternal damnation. What transpires throughout the lines of this cosmic drama which d'Aubigné explains for us is the author's tremendous belief in what he is illustrating. It is here that we find drawn together and concentrated all those characteral traits which appear separately in other works of the Huguenot literary warrior — his dynamism, his sincerity, and his desire to further the Protestant cause in the face of all adversity and against any opposition, whether it come from the pope, the king, or the Protestants themselves.

III Misères

The very tone of the opening lines stresses the inner need for d'Aubigné to express his heated feelings. By means of an extended comparison between his own mission and that of Hannibal, he sees himself destined to save the captive church. He calls upon the omniscient, omnipotent divinity to guide him and

> Puisque de ton amour mon ame est eschauffee,
> Jalouze de ton nom, ma poictrine embrazee
> De ton feu, repurge aussi de mesmes feux
> Le vice naturel de mon coeur vicieuz.
>
> (*T*, I, ll.45-48)

Since my soul is inflamed with your love, jealous of your name, my bosom burning with your fire, purge as well with the same flames the natural vice from my vicious heart.

This passage is, at the same time, a reaffirmation of Christian Calvinist modesty and a theme of Pléiade poetics which, following the Greeks, considered vice to be alien to the poetic vocation. The poet, turning his back on his previous profane poetry, insists that "Autre fureur qu'amour reluit en mon visage" (*T*, I, l.66) ("A fury other than love glows in my face"). The subject of his poem is taken from sordid, bloody reality and he invokes Melpomene, the tragic Muse, who addresses France in the most emotional, yet patriotic, manner. France is likened to a mother whose two children, like Esau and Jacob, are at war with one another and have caused her malediction. She resembles, d'Aubigné continues, a sick, monstrous giant who is in a state of corruption and decomposition. This comparison between the body politic and the human body recalls a similar development in the meditation on Psalm 133. France is also like a vessel at sea with two rival parties aboard. False laws have produced false kings, and here d'Aubigné indicates his view of the relationship between kings and their peoples:

> Les Rois, qui sont du peuple et les Rois et les peres,
> Du troupeau domestiq sont les loups sanguinaires;
> Ils sont l'ire allumee et les verges de Dieu.
>
> (*T*, I, ll.197-99).

The kings, who are both the fathers and the kings of the people, are the blood-thirsty wolves of the domestic flock, they are the burning anger and the rods of God.

A Poetic Vision—Les Tragiques

Crime is prevalent, murderers abound — a view which reflects the author's general opinion that all justice and life on earth have been reversed, for they live in a "monde à l'envers." Evil deeds on earth are rewarded not punished, people flee villages to live like animals in the forests. This concept is developed extensively and colors the whole design of the first books of *Les Tragiques*. Within this topsy-turvy world man has changed his nature: "L'homme n'est plus un homme" (*T*, I, 1.312), and his place has been taken, metaphorically speaking, by animals: "Les loups et les renards et les bestes sauvages/Tiennent place d'humains, possedent les villages" (*T*, I, ll.325-26) ("The wolves, the foxes, and the wild beasts take the place of humans, possess the villages"). There follows the contrasting picture of the poor people in the persecutions and troubles of the civil wars, suffering the pains of hell on earth, while their princes and rulers lull their consciences with lavish courtly extravaganzas. From his own experience the poet conjures up a picture of the horrors of the civil wars which as he declares in a Job-like phrase, have had an astounding effect upon him: "Mes cheveux estonnez herissent en ma teste" (*T*, I, 1.429). What a difference exists between the days of the good old kings and the present tyrants! D'Aubigné unites the two themes introduced earlier, that of the decaying body of France and that of the wicked animallike leaders, when he exclaims: "Ces tyrans sont des loups..." (*T*, I, 1.601). "Nos villes sont charongne, et nos plus cheres vies,/Et le suc et la force en ont esté ravies" (*T*, I, ll.605-6) ("These tyrans are wolves.... Our towns are carrion, and our dearest lives, both the marrow and the strength have been taken away from them"). France has brought this punishment on herself through her abandonment of the old virtue. In this way d'Aubigné adapts the Pléiade tradition to the cause of Protestantism, for already in *Les Antiquitez de Rome* du Bellay had shown how civil wars had been the reason for Rome's downfall, and Ronsard, in his "Hymne de la Justice," had developed the theme of Justice going into self-exile from earth.

In this hell that is life on earth, two evil spirits are responsible for much of the havoc: "Une fatale femme, un cardinal qui d'elle,/Parangon de mal-heur, suivoit l'ame cruelle" (*T*, I, ll.725-26) ("A fatal woman, a cardinal, a paragon of misfortune, who followed her cruel soul"). This transparent allusion to Catherine de Medici and the cardinal of Lorraine is in keeping with the general tone of the Protestant pamphleteers who chose this unhappy pair as the butt of their polemics. As is normal in sixteenth-century satire it is the monstrous qualities of the person attacked which are exaggerated, as are alleged sexual misdemeanors. The two are compared with biblical degenerates such as Jezebel and Achitophel. Catherine is accused of dabbling in black magic, of resorting to murder by poison, of fornicating with the cardinal! Similarly the cardinal was the absolute in moral corruption: "Adultere, paillard, bougre et incestueux" (*T,* I, 1.1004). Catherine was associated with the Italian influence which was so apparent in court life. D'Aubigné blames the Italians for introducing the deleterious practice of duelling which distracts men from the real art of soldiering. Italy too was blamed for the Jesuits whose subversive influence is denounced in a most powerful invective:

> Voila vostre evangile, ô vermine espagnolle,
> Je dis vostre evangile, engeance de Loyole,
> Qui ne portez la paix sous le double manteau,
> Mais qui empoisonnez l'homicide cousteau.
>
> (*T,* I, ll.1245-48)

This is your gospel, Oh Spanish vermine, I say your gospel, offspring of Loyola, who do not bring peace beneath your double coat, but who add poison to the murderous knife.

a passage illustrating d'Aubigné's skill in using all evidence to make his indictment more effective, for he is of course again referring to the attempt on Henry IV's life by Châtel.

This patriotic review of the French scene culminates in an appeal to God to consider the plight of his church. With the reaffirmation of his belief in God's goodness, d'Aubigné underlines the steadfastness of the faithful and asks God to listen to their prayer and to punish the wicked — the first book ending on a note, both biblical in pitch and so typical of the poet's own fiery nature:

> Leve ton bras de fer, haste tes pieds de laine,
> Venge ta patience en l'aigreur de la peine,
> Frappe du ciel Babel: les cornes de son front
> Desfigurent la terre et lui ostent son rond!
>
> (*T,* I, ll.1377-80).

Raise your arm of iron, hasten your feet of wool, avenge your patience in the bitterness of the punishment, strike Babel from heaven: the horns on its façade disfigure the earth and destroy its roundness.

IV Princes

The dynamic opening of *Misères* is repeated with the poet expressing his desire to attack the monstrous serpent of corruption. He also includes certain generalities about style and his conception of his work, thereby betraying his own partiality: "Je voi ce que je veux, et non ce que je puis,/Je voi mon entreprise, et non ce que je suis" (*T,* II, ll.43-44) ("I see what I want and not what I can, I see my undertaking and not what I am"). As the title of the canto suggests, the aim of d'Aubigné's satire is to denounce those in authority. He criticizes the flatterers who surround the princes, the state counsellors, for they are seduced by Satan and support their masters to further their own nefarious ends. They resort to subterfuge and substitute "paraître" for "être," they are interested in outward appearances rather than inner goodness (*T,* II, ll.206-7). God has chosen the princes to be his servants on earth, and it is up to them to live up to their responsibilities (*T,* II, ll.402-4). Alluding to the sins of Charles IX and Henry III, d'Aubigné emphasizes how God can read the hearts of men and can tell false piety from true. The good king looks after his people, the false one becomes no better than a beast when he persecutes them (*T,* II, l.495).

D'Aubigné is able to expound his theories on the good and the bad king which he elaborated in *Du Debvoir mutuel des Roys et des subjects,* and which were very much in the minds of the Protestant propagandists who sought to justify the taking up of arms by the members of their party against the crown. The perfect king is a just ruler:

> Qui establit sur soy pour roine la nature,
> Qui craint Dieu, qui esmeut pour l'affligé son coeur,
> Entrepreneur prudent, hardi executeur,
> Craintif en prosperant, dans le peril sans crainte,
> Au conseil sans chaleur, la parole sans feinte,
> Imprenable au flatteur, gardant l'ami ancien,
> Chiche de l'or public, tres-liberal du sien,
> Pere de ses subjects, ami du miserable,
> Terrible à ses haineux, mais à nul mesprisable,
> Familier, non commun, aux domestiques doux,
> Effroyable aux meschans, equitable envers tous....
> (*T,* II, ll.502-12)

Who places nature as queen over himself, who fears God, whose heart moves for the afflicted, who is prudent to undertake, bold to execute, fearful in prosperity, fearless in times of peril, passionless in counsel, honest in speech, impervious to the flatterer, who keeps his old friend, is sparing with public money and very liberal with his own, who is the father of his subjects, the friend of the wretched, a terror to those who hate him but scorned by none, friendly but not common, gentle toward his servants, frightful toward the wicked and just toward all.

Not only Montaigne but the majority of contemporary humanists would have agreed with such precepts — as did, for the most part, Ronsard in his *Institution pour l'Adolescence du Roy tres-chrestien Charles IXe de ce nom* (1562).

The privy council, d'Aubigné claims, is composed of people of doubtful morals, and the virtuous go unrewarded. Subterfuge and deception are the order of the day (*T,* II, ll.651-54). The luxurious lives of the princes stand in contrast to the suffering of the people. This lengthy moral indictment is based upon the underlying concept of *Misères,* that of a topsy-turvy world. Referring to Catherine de Medici and Henry III, the poet uses the antithetical description of "une femme hommace" and "un homme femme."

The theatrical aspect of the situation is greatly exploited, as for example when the author satirizes the penitential processions that were favored by Henry III, either in the interests of peace or of begetting an heir (*T,* II, ll.971-82). The sexual crimes which are treated with great verve, also tend to be "unnatural." Marguerite de Valois, it is suggested, has a bastard child assassinated; Henry III practices sodomy and indulges in superstitious rites. Once again, as in *Misères,* d'Aubigné supports his remarks with personal observations based upon his own experience. He recalls the time he spent at the royal court, which quickly disillusioned him. He uses personification to give substance to a vision he had — first Fortune appears and ironically offers to advise the young d'Aubigné to practice dishonesty and corruption, so as to succeed. She is followed by an impatient Virtue who gives a contrary counsel, in terms indicating that these two allegorical figures are representative of the theme of "paraître" and "être." Virtue exclaims: "Mesprise un titre vain, les honneurs superflus/Retire toi dans toi, parois moins, et sois plus" (*T,* II, ll.1373-74) ("Scorn a vain title and superfluous honors, retreat within yourself, 'appear' less and 'be' more"). After the disappearance of Virtue, the poet makes a final exhortation to the courtiers not to tolerate royal vices but to

A Poetic Vision—Les Tragiques

take a firm stand; otherwise — and here he looks forward to the final books of *Les Tragiques* — they will be punished by God (*T,* II, ll.1513-17).

Of all the cantos, it is *Princes* which has probably been inspired most by the pamphlets which abounded in France in the closing years of the sixteenth century. D'Aubigné's line of attack closely resembles theirs, but it has the advantage of forming part of his general theme and of being expressed in a way which mingles the polemic with the poetic.

V   La Chambre dorée

The shortest of the books and one of the most stylized, *La Chambre dorée* introduces another perspective. Having portrayed in the first two books the sorry state of terrestrial affairs, the author allows the reader to have a glimpse of the heavenly scene. While God sits in justice surrounded by his angelic messengers, Justice herself arrives in a sorry state, "en sueurs, pantelante, meurtrie et deschirée." She wishes to return to heaven after having been so badly treated on earth; she is followed by Piety and Peace, who have both felt obliged to accompany her. The angels appeal to God to support the faithful. They, and the sight of the martyrs who have arrived in heaven, bring anger to God's eyes. This anthropomorphic presentation of God and the heavenly host is typical of works of piety of the period and of the representation of heavenly joys in the plastic arts. The scene where God, in anger, decides to take a look at the earthly world for himself, may seem rather quaint to the modern reader:

> Dieu se leve en courroux et au travers des cieux
> Perça, passa son chef; à l'esclair de ses yeux
> Les cieux se sont fendus.
>
> (*T,* III, ll.139-41).

God rises up in anger and His head pierced and passed through the heavens; the heavens divided at the sight of the gleam in his eyes.

The Almighty, seated on a cloud, takes the decision to visit Paris and the Palais de Justice. The description which follows is remarkable for its use of horror and the macabre. The Palais de Justice is built on bones and skulls with mortar made from the ashes of the dead and human blood. Animal imagery, already well developed in the first books, is here continued and the lawyers are painted in blood-chilling colors (*T,* III, ll.197-203). Satire of justice was traditional in sixteenth-century literature and both Rabelais and Montaigne develop this theme. D'Aubigné is, however, particularly virulent, and inspired perhaps by Rabelais's technique of personifying vices, he gives a long, often wearying, list of the vices to be found in *La Chambre dorée.*

In the impressive exposition of Injustice and the twenty-seven vices who attend her, the accent is on their plastic quality. D'Aubigné talks of the "tableau" he is offering the reader. In his portraits the poet follows a well-established iconographical tradition, and the traits of his personifications are to be found in the works of many of his contemporaries. The accent is upon the vices' physical appearance and the close relationship between this and their immoral nature. The portrait of Vanity is obviously influenced by contemporary court dress and reminds one of the frontispiece to Artus Thomas's *L'Isle aux Hermaphrodites* and the chapters on fashion in the *Avantures du Baron de Faeneste:*

> Ses cheveux afriquains, les chausses en valise...
> La perruque du crin d'un honneste pendu
> Et de celui qui part d'une honteuse place.
> Le poulet enlacé autour du bras s'enlace,
> On l'ouvre aux compagnons: tout y sent la putain,
> Le geste effeminé, le regard incertain,
> Fard et ambre par tout, quoy qu'en la saincte chambre
> Le fard doit estre laid, puant doit estre l'ambre.
>
> (*T,* III, ll.398-406)

His African style hair, his baggy hose..., the wig made from the hair of an honest hanged man and of that which comes from a shameful place. The entwined love note entwines itself around his arm, it is opened for friends: all smacks of the whore, the effeminate gesture, the uncertain look, make-up and amber everywhere, despite the fact that in the sacred chamber make-up must be ugly and amber evil-smelling.

From the Palais de Justice, the Divinity moves on to Spain to the seat of the Inquisition, a veritable "abrégé de l'enfer." The author makes a diatribe against the inquisitional processions and those who support them with their silence. As in *Misères,* with the attack against the Jesuits, the remarks directed against the Inquisition are

A Poetic Vision—Les Tragiques

founded on the opposition between French national interest and corrupt foreign influence as well as on religious principles. Although mortals can be gagged the truth of heaven can never be silenced: God will mete out ultimate justice and as proof, d'Aubigné gives the description of a Triumph — not a caricature (as at the end of *Faeneste*) but one which is more reminiscent of Petrarch. The Triumph is that of "la sage Themis," the goddess of Justice, "Qui abat à ses pieds ses pervers ennemis" (*T,* III, 1.696). The "heroes" of the Old Testament lead, followed by the Greeks, Persians, Romans, and ancient French. Finally, the modern group, which is not so large as the others, appears. The enemies of Justice take to flight at the sight of the procession but do not go to Switzerland or England where Justice is sovereign. There follows an eulogy of Elizabeth I, for whom d'Aubigné had great admiration as a defender of the faith. The canto concludes with a general condemnation of the wicked who will receive their punishment from God's hands.

VI Les Feux

The structure of *Les Feux* is similar to that of *La Chambre dorée,* in that we are presented with a "tableau" of the martyrs for the faith. This tableau is further divided into two parts, devoted to the martyrs who existed before the outbreak of the Wars of Religion, and to those who followed. The procession of the faithful is presented dynamically, being in the form of a vision which occurred after the poet's initial conception of the content of the book:

> Dormant sur tel dessein, en mon esprit ravi
> J'eus un songe au matin, parmi lequel je vi
> Ma conscience en face, ou au moins son image,
> Qui au visage avoit les traits de mon visage.
>
> (*T,* IV, ll.23-26)

Going to sleep on such a plan, in my enraptured mind I had in the morning a dream, in which I saw my conscience face to face, or at least its shape, which on its countenance had the features of my own.

In compiling the list of martyrs, d'Aubigné often has recourse to Crespin's *Histoire des martyrs,* choosing the most spectacular of the deaths and relating the stoical last words of the victims. The details from time to time border upon the gruesome as in the case of Gardiner, an English martyr:

> On le traine au supplice, on coupe sa main dextre,
> Il la porte à la bouche avec sa main senestre,
> La baise; l'autre poing luy est couppé soudain,
> Il met la bouche à bas et baise l'autre main.
> (*T,* IV, ll.309-12)

He is dragged to the torture, his right hand is cut off, he bears it to his mouth with his left hand and kisses it; suddenly his other fist is cut off, he lowers his mouth and kisses the other hand.

In a *monde à l'envers,* noble qualities have been displaced, for God has changed around the attributes of the social orders "Il mit des coeurs de Rois aux seins des artisans,/Et aux cerveaux des Rois des esprits de paisans" (*T,* IV, ll.379-80) ("He places the hearts of kings in the breast of working men, and in the brains of kings the minds of country folk"). God is merciful toward those who suffer in his name, as he was toward the tennis-ball maker of Avignon who was subjected to an extraordinary form of punishment:

> logé dans une cage
> Suspendue au plus haut de la plus haute tour.
> La plus vive chaleur du plus chaud et grand jour,
> Et la nuict de l'hyver la plus froide et cuisante
> Lui furent du printemps une haleine plaisante.
> (*T,* IV, ll.394-98)

...placed in a cage suspended from the highest point of the highest tower. The most intense heat of the warmest and central part of the day, and the coldest and most penetrating cold of the winter nights were a pleasant breeze of spring for him.

The very variety of the examples prevents the monotony which was evident in the irksome rosary of vices in *La Chambre dorée*. Although these pages may not be of burning interest to modern readers, we can imagine the reaction d'Aubigné hoped for among his own contemporaries when they were confronted with an impressive picture of the steadfastness of their coreligionaries and of their remarkable patience in the face of adversity.

Virtually in the middle of the book, d'Aubigné places a statement

A Poetic Vision—Les Tragiques

of Protestant faith in the mouth of Montalchine, killed in 1553, the doctrinal points of which are elaborated in the author's "Lettre à Madame sur la douceur des afflictions." This was a good tactical and political move, if not entirely satisfying from the poetic viewpoint. The statement thus becomes the centerpiece of *Les Feux* and provides the justification of so many deaths. The "credo" revolves around three words, "seul, seule et seulement," which attach Protestant doctrine to the Bible alone, name Christ as the only mediator for our sins, and proclaim that man is justified uniquely by his faith. So many of the martyrs portrayed by d'Aubigné could have repeated with Montalchine: "Vien Evangile vray, va t'en fausse doctrine!/Vive Christ, vive Christ! et meure Montalchine!" (*T*, II, ll.705-6). ("Come true Gospel, go away false doctrine! Long live Christ! Long live Christ and let Montalchine die!").

The second part, dealing with the martyrdoms following the outbreak of the civil wars, depicts the joy of the martyrs at leaving their terrestrial burdens for the peace of heaven. The victims of persecution are made to utter moving speeches, full of exhortations to practice Christian stoicism in death. Physical suffering is to be overcome: "S'ils vous ostent vos yeux, vos esprits verront Dieu" (*T*, IV, 1.847) ("If they take away your eyes, your minds will see God"). The pathetic is also introduced in a heartrending conversation between a boy, his father, and his uncle. It is the child perhaps who shows the most courage:

> Mourons! peres, mourons! ce dit l'enfant à l'heure.
> L'homme est si inconstant à changer de demeure,
> La nouveauté lui plait; et quand il est au lieu
> Pour changer cette fange à la gloire de Dieu,
> L'homme commun se plaint!
>
> (*T*, IV, ll.953-57)

Let us die, fathers, let us die! thus spoke the child at the appointed time. Man is so inconstant about changing abode, novelty pleases him; and when he is in the position to change this filth for the glory of God, the common man laments!

The poet is in admiration before those who have stood up to the Antichrist in Rome, and he also celebrates the most recent martyrs in lines which have become famous:

> Le printemps de l'Eglise et l'esté sont passés,
> Si serez vous par moi, vers bouttons, amassés,
> Encor esclorrez-vous, fleurs si franches, si vives,
> Bien que vous paroissiez dernieres et tardives;
> On ne vous lairra pas, simples, de si grand pris,
> Sans vous voir et flairer au celeste pourpris.
> Une rose d'automne est plus qu'une autre exquise:
> Vous avez esjoui l'automne de l'Eglise.
>
> (*T,* IV, ll.1227-34)

The spring and the summer of the church have passed, and so you will live through me, green buds, clustered together, you will blossom anew, such simple, bright flowers, although you may appear last and late in the season; you will not be abandoned, flowers of such great price, without being seen and smelt in heaven. An autumn rose is more exquisite than any other: you have brightened the autumn of the church.

The Catholics felt that all would be well if the Protestants prayed to their saints, but d'Aubigné, quoting from St. Cyprian, rebuts their misguided ideas, for "Comment pourroit la mort loger dans les desirs/De ceux qui ont pour dieu la chair et les plaisirs?" (*T,* IV, ll.1343-44) ("How could death figure in the desires of those who have flesh and pleasures for their god?"). To conclude, God who has now seen enough of what is happening to the faithful, is filled with sorrow and anger. He withdraws from earth, full of regret at having created it, and although he could increase the acts of suffering to test the faithful, he decides merely to tolerate those that exist. The book finishes on lines which are full of biblical imagery, not only of Christ on the cross, but also of God's ascent into heaven, which seem to have been inspired both by Ezekiel's vision and also by the departure of Elijah borne up to heaven by a chariot of fire and a whirlwind. The departure of God is reflected in the symbolic use of light and darkness: "La terre se noircit d'espais aveuglement,/Et le ciel rayonna d'heureux contentement" (*T,* IV, ll.1419-20) ("The earth becomes dark beneath the thick covering and the heavens shine forth in happy contentment"). *Les Feux* has thus a strong structural link with *La Chambre dorée,* for it was at the beginning of Book III that God descended from heaven.

VII Les Fers

The scene is transferred once again to heaven when God takes up

A Poetic Vision—Les Tragiques

his seat in splendor. This factitious setting allows d'Aubigné to mingle the supernatural with the facts of history and to give credence to his thesis that the sufferings of the church are known to the Divinity and judged by him. Satan puts in an appearance and boasts of his achievements on earth. He claims that the martyrs are glad to die because they live in such miserable conditions. Were God to remove the hardships and allow them to taste the joys of success in battle, then the people would put their trust in the princes and not in Him. Satan asks for permission to put to the test those who proclaim their Protestant steadfastness. God agrees, but forewarns Satan that his net will only ensnare "les abandonnés/Qui furent nés pour toy premier que fussent nés" (*T,* V, ll.179-80) ("...the abandoned ones who were born for you before they were born"). The presentation of Satan's descent to wreak havoc on earth resembles that of God's in *La Chambre dorée:* "Le ciel pur se fendit, se fendant il eslance/Ceste peste du ciel aux pestes de la France" (*T,* V, ll.183-84) ("...the pure heaven splits in two, as it splits it throws this plague from heaven on to the plagues of France"). One of his first acts is to enter the body of Catherine de Medici, and he soon finds plenty of support amongst the courtiers, the counsellors, the men of the church, court ladies, and lawyers. It is she who encourages the faithful to lose patience and take up arms (*T,* V, ll.244-52). His influence extends to the Vatican, the seat of the Antichrist. The guardian angels return to heaven to reveal what they have witnessed: "Les hontes de Satan, les combats de l'Eglise" (*T,* V, 1.272) ("...the scandalous acts of Satan, the combats of the church"). D'Aubigné prepares to undertake a description of the *tableaux* they have seen, but stresses that he is acting as the instrument of God: "Dieu met en cette main la plume pour escrire/Où un jour il mettra le glaive de son ire" (*T,* V, ll.307-8) ("God places the pen to write in that hand where one day he will put the sword of his anger"). The first tableau provides the atmosphere of what is to follow. It is a blind Bellona, the goddess of war, and in her personification her body reveals the horrors of civil strife: "Ses cheveux gris, sans loy, sont grouillantes viperes/Qui lui crevent le sein, dos et ventre d'ulceres" (*T,* V, ll.331-32) ("Her grey disheveled hair is composed of swarming vipers which puncture her chest, her back, and abdomen with sores"). The poet is set on depicting all the horrors of the civil wars — the battles of Dreux, Paris, Jarnac, Montcontour, etc., are passed in review. After the battles we are introduced to the massacres, so that we can see "entre les dents des tigres les aigneaux" (*T,* V, 1.536). The chief image is that of blood which characterizes the massacres from Vassy onward. The rivers of France are replete with the gory bodies of the massacred. We are thus led up to what is the central section of *Les Fers* and indeed of *Les Tragiques,* namely, the narration of the St. Bartholomew's Day Massacre. It is presented in a particularly dramatic fashion: "Venez voir comme Dieu chastia son Eglise/Quand sur nous, non sur luy, sa force fut assise" (*T,* V, ll.705-6) ("Come and see how God punished his church when it was founded on ourselves and not on Him"); and the events of the day are highlighted with great lyricism. The theatricality of the scene is accentuated: dawn draws back the curtains of the spectacle which is watched by the heavenly sun and the people of Paris. We can sense the bitterness and the disillusionment of the true patriot when the poet proclaims his reaction to what has happened to the French capital:

> La cité où jadis la loy fut reveree,
> Qui à cause des loix fut jadis honoree,
> Qui dispensoit en France et la vie et les droicts,
> Où fleurissoyent les arts, la mere de nos Rois,
> Vid et souffrit en soy la populace armee
> Trepigner la justice, à ses pieds diffamee.
> (*T,* V, ll.793-98)

The city where once law was revered, which was once honored because of its laws, which dispensed in France both life and justice, where the arts, the mother of our kings, flourished, witnessed, and allowed the armed populace to trample down Justice, defamed at its feet.

Horrors are committed, bodies thrown in the Seine, people die showing spectacular serenity in death in spite of their suffering. Charles IX is reported to have taken a bestial pleasure in the spectacle. It is here that the material of *Princes* and of *Les Feux* coincides. We are shown the tyranny of the rulers and the patience of the faithful who are like sacrificial lambs. Here too we find the example of the inhuman conduct proclaimed in *Misères,* for as d'Aubigné states "L'homme ne fut plus homme" (*T,* V, 1.1031). Similar scenes are recalled from the massacres which spread from Paris throughout France. D'Aubigné confesses that it was at this time that he experienced the visions whence emerged *Les Tragiques:*

A Poetic Vision—Les Tragiques

> Parmi ces aspres temps l'esprit, ayant laissé
> Aux assassins mon corps en divers lieux percé,
> Par l'Ange consolant mes ameres blessures,
> Bien qu'impur, fut mené dans les regions pures.
> Sept heures me parut le celeste pourpris
> Pour voir les beaux secrets et tableaux que j'escris,
> Soit qu'un songe au matin m'ait donné ces images,
> Soit qu'en la pamoison l'esprit fit ces voyages.
> Ne t'enquiers, mon lecteur, comment il vid et fit,
> Mais donne gloire à Dieu en faisant ton profit.
> Et cependant qu'en luy, exstatic, je me pasme,
> Tourne à bien les chaleurs de mon enthousiasme.
> (*T,* V, ll.1195-206)

During these harsh times, my mind, having left my body pierced in various places, for the assassins, was led, although impure, by the Angel tending my bitter wounds into the pure regions. For seven hours heaven appeared to me so that I could see the beautiful secrets and tableaux that I describe, either a morning dream gave me these pictures, or my mind made this voyage while I was in a swoon. Do not ask, my reader, how it saw and did it, but give thanks to God by taking profit from it. While I in ecstasy, swoon in Him, make good use of the ardor of my rapture.

The passage of the tableaux through the heavens comes to an end, and the poet reminds us of the eternal book of words which is kept there and how all people will be reunited after the last resurrection. An angel confers with the author and sees in the stars the siege of La Rochelle and Sancerre by the Catholics and the behavior of the princes and the treatment they receive at the hands of others. Reference is made for example to the Journée des Barricades (1588), when Henry III was obliged to abandon his capital, and to the subsequent massacre of the Guise brothers at Blois. The author even catches sight of himself wounded and laid out on a table at Talcy. D'Aubigné sums up the lesson of what he sees thus: "Tu m'as montré, ô Dieu, que celuy qui te sert/Sauve sa vie alors que pour toy il la perd" (*T,* V, ll.1431-32) ("You have shown me, Oh God, that he who serves you saves his life when he loses it for you"). The final vision of the work has been prepared for by the frequent allusions throughout *Les Fers* to rivers bearing away the massacred dead. We are given a personified portrait of "L'Océan" who complains of the corpses which have been washed down by the rivers. The angels come down and separate the blood of the murderers from that of the murdered. The Ocean changes his tone and adds that he is not angry with the massacred but with the perpetrators of the deed (*T,* V, ll.1525-27).

In the last few lines the poet addresses the "Etrangers irrités" who have been moved by such scenes and appeals to them to come to the help of the afflicted. He advises those who are persecuting the faithful to read *Les Tragiques* through to the end, so as to learn how: "L'Eternel fait à poinct vengeance et jugement" (*T,* V, 1.1560).

VIII   Vengeances

By way of introduction to this book, there is a dramatic apostrophe in the form of an appeal to God to make his secrets known to the poet. To be able to detach one's spirit from material things and catch a glimpse of the eternal, one needs to be old, but the poet is young and full of vice. He asks God to change him:

> Change-moy, refai-moy, exerce ta pitié,
> Rens moy mort en ce monde, oste la mauvaistié
> Qui possede à son gré ma jeunesse premiere;
> Lors je songeray songe et verray ta lumiere.
> (*T,* VI, ll.35-38)

Change me, make me again, exercise your mercy, make me dead to this world, remove the wickedness which does as it wishes with my early youth; then I shall dream a dream and I shall see your light.

Similarly, one has to be a child to have visions, because in this state the body is free of vice. He calls upon God to waken him from the dead, to replace his tongue with a tongue of fire and incite in him the qualities he seeks: "Les songes d'un vieillard, les fureurs d'un enfant" (*T,* VI, 1.64) ("The dreams of an old man, the furies of a child"). The reader should not expect to discover fictitious representations of God's truth but factual ones. The poet describes how the spirit has moved him, has changed him into a new man. In a confession of his sins, he admits to having wasted his youth, to having been a slave to kings and vanity, to having stifled the truth, but, like Jonah, he has been saved from great dangers. The analogy with Jonah is not gratuitous, because d'Aubigné sees himself in the same prophetic role, for God has stirred him also to fight against the contemporary Nineveh. Throughout the description of the way

A Poetic Vision—Les Tragiques

in which God has punished the persecutors of the church the role of Satan is well indicated.

We find in this book the heart of the doctrinal argument of *Les Tragiques*. The center of *Les Fers* was the St. Bartholomew's Day Massacre, which was the most important physical event in the persecution of the Protestants; in *Vengeances* we are presented with the main ideological conflict. D'Aubigné sees a symbolic precursor of the St. Bartholomew's Day Massacre in the first murder on record, that of Abel by Cain. He had already cited the dispute between Jacob and Esau as an early example of the differences between the churches, but with Cain and Abel we are faced with the archetype:

> De Caïn fugitif et d'Abel je veux dire
> Que le premier bourreau et le premier martyre,
> Le premier sang versé on peut voir en eux deux:
> L'estat des agneaux doux, des loups outrecuideux.
> En eux deux on peut voir (beau portrait de l'Eglise)
> Comme l'ire et le feu des ennemis s'attise
> De bien fort peu de bois et s'augmente beaucoup.
> (*T*, VI, ll.157-63)

I mean that you can see in the fugitive Cain and Abel the first executioner and the first martyr, the first bloodshed: the state of the gentle lambs, of the presumptuous wolves. In them you can see (a beautiful portrait of the church) how the anger and fire of enemies is kindled with very little wood and spreads enormously.

The quarrel between the two brothers was provoked by jealousy, and Cain was severely punished by the Almighty. From this primeval source d'Aubigné traces the way in which God works. He traverses the major episodes of the Old Testament, mentioning the tower of Babel, Sodom and Gomorrah, etc., constantly making the correlation between past and present. Saul is described as having been possessed by hatred, and d'Aubigné immediately creates a parallel between the Old Testament king and the contemporary rulers who persecute the Protestant Davids (*T*, VI, ll.331-34). Like the princes in the second book, Nebuchadnezzar has lost his human nature: "Ce Roy n'est donc plus Roy, de prince il n'est plus prince" (*T*, VI, 1.393). The review of the persecutors places the accent on the horror of their suffering. Herod is eaten away by worms, as was the sixteenth-century Pope Paul IV, and also Philip II of Spain. D'Aubigné turns his attention to the attackers of the early church such as Nero, who, like Nebuchadnezzar, was inhuman in his conduct: "Homme tu ne fus point à qui t'avoit fait homme' (*T,* VI, 1.529). The list of tyrannical emperors is an impressive one, and one of the most dastardly in the poet's mind is the Emperor Julian the Apostate, who was much maligned in the sixteenth century.

The third group of persecutors are said to be direct descendants of Julian and represent those who pursued the Reformers. The past/present analogy is continuously in evidence, but now it is the present which is compared with the past. The worms which tormented Herod are recalled when the poet refers to the massacre of Merindol:

> Qui veut sçavoir comment la vengeance divine
> A bien sçeu où dormoit d'Herode la vermine
> Pour en persecuter les vers persecuteurs,
> Qu'il voye le tableau d'un des inquisiteurs
> De Merindol en feu.
>
> (*T,* VI, ll.821–25)

Who wants to know how divine vengeance knew where Herod's vermine was dormant so as to persecute the persecuting worms with them, let him see the picture of one of the inquisitors of Merindol in flames.

It is the hand of God which has ordained such punishments. The whole message of the book is to warn the wicked of the fate that is in store for them and to bring comfort to the afflicted. We have the clear impression that the persecutors have been deceived by the devil, and d'Aubigné stresses this in his description of the death of the papal legate, Marcel Crescentio, for: "L'air, noirci de demons ainsi que de nuages,/ Creva des quatre parts d'impetueux orages" (*T,* VI, ll.1045–46) ("The air, blackened with demons as well as clouds, burst out in all four parts with raging thunderstorms"). These incidents are not pure coincidence, the poet claims; they are the manifestation of God's intervention in human affairs. The poet comes to a sudden halt through fear of wearying his reader and states again that he is not writing for the "serfs de la vanité" but for the "enfans de verité." God has now changed his methods; for once he came to the help of his church in danger by succoring the innocent, but now: "Il marche à la vengeance et non plus au secours" (*T,* VI, 1.1132).

IX Jugement

The initial movement is similar to that of the previous book, with the poet invoking the Divinity to visit the earth with his wrath, punish those who hate Him, and instill in the hearts of the faithful "the fear of the Lord." D'Aubigné is the intermediary as Ananias was to Paul: "Ambassadeur portant et la veuë et la vie" (*T,* VII, ll.26). On the one hand, the faithful will be rewarded in heaven and on the other, the wicked will be punished. We now attain the climax of the spiritual message that the poet has been proclaiming throughout the preceding books of the poem. With visionary clarity, he imagines the "faux marchands," the "Maquignons de Satan," the "apostats degeneres." From the ranks of the ordinary folk his invective rises to direct itself against the descendants of the Bourbons, notably Henry IV who had turned Catholic, against tyrants, against apostate princes. To give credence to his vision of the future, the author, using the Book of Deuteronomy, repeats God's threatening words to the wicked:

> Vous qui persecutez par fer mon heritage,
> Vos flancs ressentiront le prix de vostre ouvrage,
> Car je vous frapperay d'espais aveuglemens,
> Des playes de l'Egypte et de forcenemens.
>
> (*T,* VII, ll.223-26).

You who persecute with fire my inheritance, your flanks will feel the recompense of your work, for I will strike you with thick clouds, the plagues of Egypt and mad fury.

The pains inflicted will be of a corporal nature, and the author departs on a long digression to prove that there will be a resurrection of the body. Man has been given the gift of reason and when death dissolves his body it does not destroy it, for the immortal seed remains for the resurrection. After this philosophical examination, during which the poet parades his knowledge of the Scriptures, he introduces the central element, the theme of the Last Judgment, in a typically dramatic manner. With the emphasis on the visual, we are made to feel that we are looking at some moving picture based on a painting by Hieronymous Bosch:

> Mais quoy! c'est trop chanté, il faut tourner les yeux
> Esblouis de rayons dans le chemin des cieux.

> C'est fait, Dieu veut regner, de toute prophetie
> Se void la periode à ce poinct accomplie.
> La terre ouvre son sein, du ventre des tombeaux
> Naissent des enterrés les visages nouveaux:
> Du pré, du bois, du champ, presque de toutes places
> Sortent les corps nouveaux et les nouvelles faces.
> Ici les fondemens des chasteaux rehaussés
> Par les ressuscitans promptement sont percés;
> Ici un arbre sent des bras de sa racine
> Grouïller un chef vivant, sortir une poictrine....
>
> (*T*, VII, ll.661-72)

But what? I have gone on too long, we must turn our eyes, dazzled by the rays of light, toward the path of heaven. It is done, God wishes to reign, the period of all prophecy is seen to be completed at this point. The earth opens up its bosom, from the belly of the tombs the new faces of the buried people are born: from the meadow, the wood, the field, almost from every place emerge new bodies and new faces. Here the raised foundations of the château are promptly pierced by the resurrecting people; here a tree feels with the arms of its roots a seething living head, an emerging chest....

This plastic quality is maintained throughout — the son of God and man is presented, the trumpet sounds, God appears: "Tout l'air n'est qu'un soleil" (*T*, VII, 1.721). An Archangel announces: "Venez respondre icy de toutes actions,/L'Eternel veut juger" (*T*, VII, ll.726-27) ("Come and answer here for all actions, the Eternal wants to judge"). Before the messenger of eternal death the elements seek their revenge on those who have misused them. The main satirical and doctrinal themes of the other books here find their resolution. The persecutors are the "Caïns fugitifs"; the Antichrist is responsible for unnatural crimes: "Les pechés où nature est tournée à l'envers" (*T*, VII, 1.813); not only materialism, sexual misdemeanors, but satanic aberrations, idolatry, etc.

God metes out just rewards to the good and the bad. The incessant suffering of the wicked is portrayed in baroque detail with anthropomorphic realism, which is exaggerated to enhance the contrast with heaven, for "...de ce dur estat le poinct plus ennuyeux/C'est de savoir aux enfers ce que l'on faict aux cieux" (*T*, VII, ll.1045-46) ("...of this hard state the most troublesome thing is to know in hell what is going on in heaven"). The antithetical nature of the comparison between heaven and hell fits in with the author's message of consolation to the faithful. If he has stressed throughout the topsy-turvy nature of the world, it is to show that paradoxically real life in the real world where Justice and joy exist is after mortal death (*T,* VII, ll.1097-100). The tableau's effect is somewhat weakened by its excessive detail such as the author's considerations on whether we remember earthly things in heaven. But his eulogistic description of Paradise reaches a fine climax in lines which continue the poetic and doctrinal aspects of *Les Tragiques,* for the two are constantly at each other's service:

> Au visage de Dieu seront nos saincts plaisirs,
> Dans le sein d'Abraham fleuriront nos desirs,
> Desirs, parfaits amours, hauts desirs sans absence,
> Car les fruicts et les fleurs n'y font qu'une naissance.
> (*T,* VII, ll.1205-8)

In the face of God will be our sacred pleasures, in Abraham's bosom will flower our desires — desires, perfect loves, lofty desires without an end — for fruits and flowers are born there but once.

Then with lines which evoke the stylized opening of *Les Tragiques,* as the poet recalls the similarity between the divine fury which inspires him and the pagan inspiration of the ancients, he creates a note of unity, for his poem is finished and he is exhausted:

> Mes sens n'ont plus de sens, l'esprit de moy s'envole,
> Le coeur ravi se taist, ma bouche est sans parole:
> Tout meurt, l'ame s'enfuit, et reprenant son licu
> Exstatique se pasme au giron de son Dieu.
> (*T,* VII, ll.1215-18)

My senses have no more feeling, my spirit is fleeing from me, my enraptured heart falls silent, my mouth is speechless: everything dies, the soul is escaping, and taking up its place again in ecstasy swoons in God's lap.

The poet, by his personal involvement and his narrative presence, provides the unified cadre. Although the work is divided up into books we can see that like acts in a play they form a definite part in a structure. They offer us a series of tableaux of the present, the past and the future, of earth and of heaven. Each book too is constructed on the tableau principle with the poet stressing the visual and plastic aspect of his description. We can criticize him for being long winded, for being carried away by his inspiration, but one cannot deny the beauty of the poet's conception nor the magnificence of much of the verse.

X *An Epic Poem?*

The term "epic" is rather ambiguous, and it has even been used to describe certain novels. It is generally accepted, however, that the epic is a long narrative poem recounting heroic deeds. For the man of the Renaissance the models of such a poem were to be found in the works of Homer and Virgil. The most striking difference that exists in the case of d'Aubigné is that he has based his poem apparently on fact rather than on legend. Can such a practice be justified? To a certain extent, Homer, Virgil, and Ronsard believed in the relative truth of the story they were narrating in a mythical guise, for it is the poet's right to use history and present it in a way different from that of the historiographer.[7] Ronsard in his *Au lecteur* of *La Franciade* (1572) had stressed the difference between the two genres:

The historian must deduce his work from point to point, from the beginning to the end, where the poet, leading to the end and unraveling the thread in a counter current to history, borne along by poetic fury and art and ... above all favored by foresight and natural judgment, proceeds so that the end of his work is closely linked to the beginning.[8]

Les Tragiques fits nicely into this definition of the poetic treatment of history, and the poem can therefore be considered an epic in Pléiade terms. In another preface to the *Franciade, Au lecteur apprentif,* Ronsard had also enumerated other qualities which he sought in the epic. The style should be poetic and not prosaic: in spite of some clumsily constructed alexandrines d'Aubigné's verse is not only poetic in structure and vocabulary but also in its conception. Ronsard recommends the provision of details and descriptions of wars; and this is only too real an aspect of *Les Tragiques* where the horrors of the civil wars are depicted with an often startling vividness in the conflict between God and man. When Ronsard referred to divine intervention, he was thinking of the gods of classical mythology; but for d'Aubigné there can be no other force than that of the Christian God who intervenes in human affairs and is the dominating presence throughout *Les Tragiques*. It is suggested by Ronsard that the poem should begin *in medias res;* this is indeed the case of the d'Aubigné work, with the first book, *Misères,* providing a picture of the present state of France which is placed in time between the original crime committed by Cain and the trials of the Day of Judgment. The prince of poets informs us that the narration should progress through the use of events, conversations, dreams, prophecies, and "peintures," all of which elements find their reflection in d'Aubigné's own poem. One might even claim that when d'Aubigné bases his text on the Bible he is following Ronsard's advice to use "quelques vieilles annales du temps passé."

If one accepts the above criteria, then it is clear that *Les Tragiques* may be considered a Christian epic. Nor must we overlook the strong oral element in *Les Tragiques,* a quality it shares with the great epics of earlier times. D'Aubigné makes constant reference to his own visual experience, and the author addresses the reader, often with a curt imperative, thereby involving him closely in the drama he is enacting. The reader thus ceases to be a spectator and becomes a participant.

XI The View of History

Compared with the Virgilian epic, it is apparent that *Les Tragiques* reveals a different conception of history on the part of the author. As T.M. Greene has pointed out, d'Aubigné has interpreted history in Christian terms. Whereas Virgil's view was based on an ideal of dynastic power, d'Aubigné saw history as a pattern of recurrences with fixed terminal limits — Creation and Judgment. The Virgilian view allows man to make some progress and improve his condition; for d'Aubigné, "the Christian pattern limited direct divine intervention to the two termini of history and to the incarnation (which plays no role in *Les Tragiques*). No more was necessary because God's will ultimately controlled a man's role and limited his capacity for earthly transcendence."[9]

D'Aubigné translates the past, present, and future in divine terms. On the one hand, there is the perfection of God in all His goodness and justice, on the other, there is mankind; and although men may come and men may go, evil, since the Fall, goes on forever. The examples of the punishment meted out by God to wrongdoers in the past serve as an explanation of the contemporary troubles which beset France, and they herald the retribution to come.

D'Aubigné's attitude to history was shared by Chassanion de Monistrol who published in 1581 a little book entitled, *Des Grands et Redoutables Jugemens et Punitions de Dieu*,[10] which provided one of the sources for the lists of punishments reserved for wrongdoers which were poeticized by d'Aubigné in *Vengeances*. In his preface, Chassanion clearly states his conception of the use of history:

History is useful and profitable to us, in that telling us the truth about past events which would otherwise remain buried in silence, it proposes us good and evil, vice and virtue, the punishment and reward of the just and the wicked.... But the true use must be such, to note diligently the effects of God's providence and of His justice, to learn how to remain humble and to fear the Lord, seeing that those who have shown in their lives, honesty, justice, temperance, and other natural virtues, have been spared in some way, and that the others have fallen into ruin, earning the punishment for their injustices.

The history of the true church is linked in *Les Tragiques* with biblical precedents in the Old Testament; Cain and Abel *(Vengeances)* are the prime symbols of the struggle between the true and the false churches. The poet explains the present in terms of the past and there are constant parallels between Old Testament events and personages and contemporary ones. Catherine de Medici is compared with Jezebel *(Misères)*, the cardinal of Lorraine with Achitophel *(Misères)*, Charles IX with Nebuchadnezzar *(Vengeances)*, and the fate that awaits France is likened to that of Sodom and Gomorrah *(Vengeances)*, etc. As the reader of sixteenth-century polemical pamphlets realizes, these analogies between the characters of the Bible and contemporary events were greatly exploited[11] and formed part of the rhetorical tradition in works of a satirical nature. They have the added value in *Les Tragiques* of serving d'Aubigné's ideological purpose. Calvin, in his *Institution chrétienne* (Chapter VII), had taught that the difference between the Old and the New Testament was that truth in the Old Testament is revealed through the "images."

Alongside the biblical references are others to figures of antiquity: some, such as the comparison with Hannibal in the opening lines of *Misères,* or the stoicism of Seneca in *Les Feux*, are to be explained by the author's humanist background; others are to be linked with the general historical perspective of the work. Nero is quoted not only as the most notorious of tyrants but also as one of the first persecutors of Christianity: other emperors, Domitian, Hadrian, Julian the Apostate, etc., are invoked as bearing witness to the way in which God punishes his opponents and as a warning to d'Aubigné's contemporary rulers. It was important for him to limit his illustrations to the early years of the church, for the Protestants maintained the church had become corrupt from the fifth century of our era onward.

Thus by his skilful use of an established literary technique, namely analogy, d'Aubigné has injected into his poem an important dimension of time. His constant switching from one point in time to another serves to underline the concept of the immutability of God, of His eternal, timeless nature. We gain the impression that d'Aubigné's view of history is that it is only the outside, the "paraître," that changes; the real nature of man, his "être," remains constant. Such a philosophy allows progress to be made only by the chosen few and gives little chance of salvation to the rest.

XII *The View of Man*

Closely connected with the author's fundamentally Christian view of history is the attitude he adopts toward man. Man is presented with all his weaknesses and at the same time, in the description of the martyrs for the faith, with all his qualities. Whether a man can be considered worthy or not depends upon the Christian criteria that d'Aubigné possesses. If a person becomes guilty of persecuting the Protestants, then it is obvious that he has been abandoned by God and is on the path of perdition. This division of the world into the good and the wicked is no doubt too categorical for our contemporary taste, but for the puritanical and fanatical d'Aubigné there was but one true religion, that of the Reformed church.

One of the essential concepts present in his description of the state of contemporary France is that his compatriots are behaving in a manner which ill befits the children of God. Through his conduct man has betrayed his human dignity, "l'homme n'est plus un homme" (*T,* I, 1.312), and on this idea is constructed a view of the world which permeates all seven books of *Les Tragiques*.[12] Rigorous logic is exercized: if a man is no longer a man then what is he? He has reverted to the animal state, "Les loups et les renards et les bestes sauvages tienent place d'humains" (*T,* I, ll.325-26). This explains the leitmotiv which runs through the epic, that of the opposition between the lambs and the wolves, between the innocent and their wicked oppressors. The latter are equally described as tigers or dogs, and Nebuchadnezzar is said to dwell among the toads and reptiles. D'Aubigné feels he is living in a topsy-turvy world, "un monde à l'envers" (*T,* I, 1.235); to prove it, he quotes the life-style of those about him, whether it be internecine strife at family level during the civil wars, the unnatural sexual conduct of Henry III, or the perversions of the Antichrist.

The reversal of normal values has been effected by the evil nature of man and by the work of the Devil. The presence of the Prince of Darkness is prominent in d'Aubigné's universe. We know that toward the end of the sixteenth century the civil and religious disorders were associated with demonic influences, and it was no mere coincidence that with the rise in accusations of heresy there was an accompanying increase in the number of people convicted of sorcery and of soliciting with the Devil.

The Devil has an important role in the poem and tries to match his force against that of God *(Les Fers).* There are glimpses of his successes with certain mortal souls: Catherine de Medici is "compagne des demons compagnons imposteurs" (*T,* I, 1.900), the Jesuits spread "le feu d'Enfer" (*T,* I, 1.1254), the king is surrounded by the Devil's disciples (*T,* II, ll.103-110), and the princes have perfected the art of disguising the devil as an angel of light (*T,* II, 1.952).

At times, the religious wars take on a Manichean dimension as d'Aubigné sees within them a struggle between the forces of good and evil. Just as the topsy-turvy state of things will be righted in God's world, so an appropriate fate awaits those who have betrayed God in this life and enjoyed the fruits of a materialistic existence: "Les tyrans abatus, pasles et criminels,/Changent leurs vains honneurs aux tourmens eternels" (*T,* VII, ll.741-42) ("The pale and criminal tyrants who have been struck down change their vain honors for eternal torment").

This tendency to see the world as a conflict between two forces is emphasized by the author's overpowering partiality. The supporters of the Protestant cause are opposed constantly to the

A Poetic Vision—Les Tragiques

Catholic forces. The former are in the camp of the saints, the latter are under the influence of Satan and are therefore to be condemned to everlasting torment.

The great accent placed upon the Devil and all his works is more a reflection of the period in which d'Aubigné lived than of his Protestantism. Both the Protestant and the Catholic opponents of the French kings used similar arguments to discredit the monarchy, and show that by their behavior the kings had ceased to behave like kings and that therefore they could be opposed and deposed with impunity. D'Aubigné's originality in this poem is not so much in his use of the established conceit that some men were abandoned by God and had lived like animals, but rather in the way he turns it against the Catholics (who, incidentally, used similar arguments against the Protestants) and creates around it a unified attack on the Catholic church, making it into a linking theme for all seven books.

Although d'Aubigné's intense feelings on the subject of religious persecution may be understandable, it must be admitted that the constant repetition of the same tenets, the same oppositions can be somewhat tedious. In spite of the splendor of certain poetic developments it is often rather wearying to find the same juxtapositions appearing within each book with a predictable regularity. And yet, the very frequence of their use may be part of d'Aubigné's polemical scheme. He wants to "move" his reader and, by showing the conflict between good and evil which has existed on every level of society since time immemorial, he hopes to convey the beauty and the justification of the true religion, that of the Protestants.

XIII The Objectives of the Satire and the Method

Les Tragiques is as much a glorification of Protestantism as it is a severe condemnation of the opponents of that religion. Almost all aspects of sixteenth-century society are attacked. Much of the vituperation is directed, however, at those in authority: the king, the courtiers, the princes who still had a great deal of territorial and political power. Justice too comes under fire as does, of course, the Roman Catholic church and all those who support the alleged Antichrist, especially the Jesuits, who are frequently reviled by the militant d'Aubigné.

His method is an impressive one. He gives credence to his remarks by stressing the veracity of what he narrates and by the very fact that he claims to have seen a vision or witnessed the details. In *Misères* he employs a technique of pathetic contrast by means of an humiliating tableau of the present state of France as compared with what it was in the past when it had good kings. Rhetorical appeals to the reader,

> Quel antre caverneux, quel sablon, quel desert,
> Quel bois, au fond duquel le voyageur se perd,
> Est exempt de mal-heurs?
>
> (*T*, I, ll.835-37)

What cavernous lair, what sandy stretch, what desert, what wood in the depths of which the traveler becomes lost, is free of misfortune?

immediately play upon his emotional responses and encourage him to be sympathetic toward the cause, whereas the rulers are handled with great severity. They are described with harsh epithets, their misdeeds are narrated at length, their moral behavior is criticized to the point of becoming at times almost a caricature, and the analogies that are drawn between them and historical precedents only help to blacken the general picture. There exists too a certain patriotic appeal: the Jesuits are the "vermine espagnolle" (*T*, I, l.1245), France is portrayed in pitiful terms: "O France desolee! ô terre sanguinaire,/Non pas terre, mais cendre!" (*T*, I, ll.89-90) ("Oh desolate France! Oh blood-thirsty earth, not earth but ashes!").

Elsewhere the satire is more oblique, as in the case of the personification of the vices in *La Chambre dorée,* or even more indirect by subtle implication such as in the juxtaposition of events and books. The portraits of the martyrs in *Les Feux* are resplendent with saintly patience, in direct opposition to those of their bestial oppressors whose ugly deaths are narrated in *Vengeances.* The Protestants possess the same stoical firmness of character and are at least the equals, if not the superiors, of those great heroes of antiquity: their speech is of a heartrending simplicity and underlines the conviction of their faith. In *Les Fers,* the magnanimity of Colligny is highlighted by the contrasting savage brutality of the massacres on St. Bartholomew's Day. Charles IX, on the other hand, is presented in horribly sinister terms. Drawing very much upon contemporary material, he weaves his attacks against the kings into a definite scheme which is to be interpreted in the light of biblical truth. The effect of the satire is full of impact, although it is to be regretted that here, as elsewhere, d'Aubigné did not prove more flexible in his attitude. To wish this is perhaps to betray the author, for he himself could never admit to any form of compromise, either political or religious.

XIV *The Style*

A number of authors in recent years have turned their attention to the style of *Les Tragiques,* and they provide a more comprehensive study than can be attempted in this brief survey.[13] Much of d'Aubigné's own personality and the flavor of an epoch are revealed in the lines of his poem. From what has preceded, it is evident that antithesis is widely employed in *Les Tragiques:* whether it be on the doctrinal level in the opposition between good and evil, God and Satan; on the political, between Protestants and Catholics, the people and their princes; or on the purely stylistic and structural levels. The basic structure of the poem is that of a series of tableaux which contrast one with another, *Misères* with *Princes* and *La Chambre dorée, Vengeances* with *Jugement.* Within the various books further contrasts are established: in *jugement,* we are provided with details of the different faes that await the good and the evil. In the actual style of the narration the role of antithesis is even greater. D'Aubigné has created a system of opposing symbolic terms which trigger in the mind of the reader a reaction similar to that established by the use of antithesis in Petrarchan love poetry where the "icy fire" range of conceits is particularly abundant.[14] For instance, there is the animal terminology, and since we know that for our author the "dehumanized" human becomes an animal, anyone described as a "ferocious beast" is to be condemned: Catherine de Medici is a "sauvage et carnasciere beste" (*T,* I, 1.810), the tyrants are coupled with the "furieuses bestes" (*T,* VII, 1.775). Elsewhere the Christian lambs are seen to be hunted by the Catholic wolves, and this persecution is traced back to the Cain and Abel episode which portrayed "L'estat des agneaux doux, des loups outrecuideux" (*T,* VI, 1.160).

The antithetical use of moral references is effective, the technique having as its origin a point of doctrine which colors the presentation of *Les Tragiques,* for d'Aubigné saw God's grace working in complete opposition to earthly honors. We therefore find that the Protestants are associated with saintly qualities, whereas the Catholics are linked with all the most horrid moral turpitudes. The presentation of these is often made in subtle fashion and can be most impressive. Henry III is described as having "le geste effeminé, l'oeil d'un Sardanapale" (*T,* II, 1.776) and the portrait reaches a climax with an antithetical construction:

> Son visage de blanc et de rouge empasté
> Son chef tout empoudré nous monstrerent ridee,
> En la place d'un Roy, une putain fardee.
>
> (*T,* II, ll.782-84)

His face caked with white and red, his head covered with powder, showed us in the place of a king, a wrinkled made-up whore.

This "surprise" technique occurs often and, with negative constructions such as "L'homme ne fut plus homme" (*T,* V, 1.1031) and "Ce Roy n'est donc plus Roy, de prince il n'est plus prince" (*T,* VI, 1.393), or ironic statements which are obviously contrary to what is normally expected. Fortune explains to the young d'Aubigné that others have succeeded by finding "Par le cul d'un coquin chemin au coeur d'un Roy" (*T,* II, 1.1318). And in the same book the poet criticizes Henry III's penitent processions which: "Ont pour masque le froc, pour vestemens des poches..." (*T,* II, ll.979).

D'Aubigné, like his contemporaries, makes extensive use of wordplay. It has become customary to reject the pun as being of particularly bad taste. This view did not prevail at the end of the sixteenth century, where the juxtaposition of two homographs, often antonyms, was a means of parading one's intellectual awareness and the paradox of language. Our author creates within *Les Tragiques* a network of words which oppose or complement one another. Sometimes it is for emphasis: "La France avoit mestier/Que ce potier fut Roy, que ce Roy fust potier (*T,* IV, ll.1251-52); or: "Retire toi dans toi, parois moins, et sois plus" (*T,* II, 1.1374). In *Les Feux* Montalchine's speech centers around "seul, seule et seulement" (*T,* IV, ll.655-706) which are the keystones to his credo. The repetition of a word sometimes reflects the rhetorical style of the author:

> C'est assez pour mourir que de pouvoir mourir,
> Il faut faire gouster les coups de la tuerie
> A ceux qui n'avoyent pas encor gousté la vie.
>
> (*T,* V, ll.620-22)

It is enough to die to be able to die, you have to make those who had not yet tasted life taste the blows of murder.

and serve to make the reader stop and ponder the meaning of a line, thereby making it more rewarding: "La mort morte ne peut vous tuer, vous saisir" (*T,* VII, 1.1014). That the author considered repetition and puns highly can be seen from the fact that he uses them frequently and in what might be considered the most important parts of the text. On the subject of Cain's punishment, he writes, "Vif il ne vescut point, mort il ne mourut pas" (*T,* VI, 1.200); and in the midst of the description of the St. Bartholomew's Day Massacre we find: "Jour qui avec horreur parmi les jours se conte,/Qui se marque de rouge et rougit de sa honte" (*T,* V, ll.769-70) ("A day which is to be counted with horror among the days, which is marked by red and blushes with shame").

This last quotation raises another interesting antithesis in *Les Tragiques,* that of color symbolism. Few adjectives of color are deployed, and those which recur constantly are red, white, black, and "pale." Red is associated with hell, punishment, battles, and shame; white with beauty and purity; whereas "pale" is an absence of color linked with death; and black represents moral degradation and complete condemnation on the part of the author. The passage describing the St. Bartholomew Day Massacre constitutes a good example of the use of symbolic colors. The day, as it breaks, is tinged with black, then it is colored by red, the sun shows its pale face rather reluctantly, etc. In this way d'Aubigné provides a symbolic premonition of the disaster to come and one which is understandable to the reader because of the use already made of the color adjectives in the previous lines.

The reduction of the color scheme to such a small number of epithets can be attributed to the visionary nature of the work. If d'Aubigné actually wrote down the products of his "inner eye," then it would be normal to expect him not to use the full color spectrum. It is difficult for some people to imagine in color, and in *Les Tragiques* certain distinctive and contrasting hues stand out amid the wealth of detail. Great emphasis is laid upon the visual element of the work, with both the author and his characters repeating that they can see what is happening: "Car mes yeux sont tesmoins du subjet de mes vers" (*T*, I, 1.371); "Je voi ce que je veux, et non ce que je puis" (*T*, II, l.43); "Vous les verrez depeints au tableau que voici" (*T*, III, 1.248); "J'eus un songe au matin, parmi lequel je vis/Ma conscience en face..." (*T*, IV, ll.24-25); "Et les premiers objects de ces yeux saints et beaux/Furent au rencontrer de ces premiers tableaux" (*T*, V, 1.325-26); "Ces fermes visions, ces veritables songes" (*T*, VI, 1.66); "Ambassadeur portant et la veuë et la vie" (*T*, VII, 1.26).

The description of France's sufferings is effected with great pathos: the wickedness of the princes and their entourage is materialized, the flatterers become vipers, the courtly rite a farce. To increase the ignominy of the persecutors of the Protestant faith and to augment the beauty of the sacrifice of the Protestant martyrs, the author often stresses the macabre nature and horror of certain acts, dwelling on the bloody details so as to move his audience. In *Les Feux* the narration of the deaths of the martyrs spares us no unpleasantness, as in the description of Gardiner's death (*T*, IV, ll.309-15). On occasions the author allows his polemic enthusiasm to run away with him, and in his enumeration of the vices, or for that matter of the qualities, there is a dominating note of exaggeration which does not enhance the poet's argument. Whenever he attacks the Roman church, all the old shibboleths are regurgitated:

> Voici donc, Antechrist, l'extraict des faits et gestes:
> Tes fornications, adulteres, incestes,
> Les pechés où nature est tournée à l'envers,
> La bestialité, les grands bourdeaux ouvers,
> Le tribut exigé, la bulle demandée
> Qui a la sodomie en esté concedée....
>
> (*T*, VII, ll.811-16)

Here is then, Oh Antichrist, the extract of your deeds and acts, your fornications, adulteries, incests, the sins where nature is turned upside down, bestiality, great houses of prostitution opened, tribute demanded, the bull solicited which granted sodomy in summer.

This procedure of exaggeration can also spoil the balance of a book and its general effect. In *Jugement,* the long exposition of the immortality of the soul wearies most modern readers, as does the accumulation of examples in *Les Feux* or the personification of vices in *La Chambre dorée*. We should not, however, condemn d'Aubigné too hastily for such accumulations for, although they may be frowned upon today, they are an essential part of the rhetorical literary process as it was understood at the end of the sixteenth century. Nourished on humanism, d'Aubigné composes his arguments in *Les Tragiques* along the lines of a Montaigne in his early essays or a Guillaume Bouchet in *Les Serées*.

The use of personification in *La Chambre dorée, Misères, Princes,* and *Les Fers,* is not just a relic of the Middle Ages but is characteristic of virtually all the great poets of d'Aubigné's time. In the same way as God is anthropomorphized, so are virtues and vices. The relationship between painting and poetry in the sixteenth century was very prominent, as was the emphasis on the allegory and the symbol. Many of the attributes employed by d'Aubigné are common currency among his contemporaries, and it is often informative to see how others explained them. In *La Chambre dorée,* Envy is described:

> L'on void en l'autre siege estriper les serpents,
> Les crapaux, le venin entre les noires dents
> Du conseiller suivant: car la mimorte Envie
> Sort des rochers hideux et traine là sa vie.
>
> (*T,* III, ll.279-82)

In the other seat can be seen disemboweling serpents and toads, the venom between the black teeth of the next counsellor: for half-dead Envy emerges from the ugly rocks and spins her life out there.

Envy is thus associated with ugliness and serpents. If we consult the *Iconology* of Cesare Ripa, which was published in Rome in 1593, we find that in his description of Envy he speaks of

> ...the figure of an old ugly woman, dressed in black and blue tarnished drapery; she is crowned with serpents: a viper is biting her left breast, which is bare, and her right hand is resting on the head of a Hydra. She is old and ugly, to signify the deformity of this vice; and the discolored drapery alludes to the vileness of an envious disposition. Her head is surrounded with serpents, to signify the evil thoughts which continually revolve in the envious mind, to the detriment of others. The viper biting her left breast, denotes the species of rage and torment that perpetually perplex the breast of those who envy the prosperity of their neighbour...."[15]

Such descriptions suggest that *La Chambre dorée* would have been more readily comprehensible to d'Aubigné's contemporaries than to us.

Whether it be through the accumulative wealth of detail or through the swiftly moving tableaux, there is running through the poem a certain pulsation of life. We are conscious of looking not at a static picture, at a still life, but at a moving image. The very force of the verbs employed by the poet helps to create this impression of dynamism. The dramatic presentation of certain scenes, the idea that the reader is taking part in the drama rather than taking a seat as a spectator, all help to make the reading of *Les Tragiques* a memorable experience. The suppression of coordination, which at times can lead to syntactic confusion, adds to the raciness of the *récit,* especially when coupled with very short phrases and in the form of a dialogue between author and reader:

> Venez voir comme Dieu chastia son Eglise
> Quand sur nous, non sur luy, sa force fut assise,
> Quand, devenus prudens, la paix et nostre foy
> Eurent pour fondement la promesse du Roy.
>
> (*T,* V, ll.705–8).

Come and see how God punished his church when on us and not on Him its strength was placed, when, after becoming prudent, peace and our faith were based upon the promise of the king.

Throughout there is a strong religious overtone and the poetry is often colored with biblical references so inserted into the text as to appear to come from the prophet d'Aubigné rather than from the Bible. All in all d'Aubigné has made full use of the rhetorical tropes at his disposition. He has succeeded in creating a majestic, vivid, and truly heroic style well befitting the subject of his poem.

In spite of the qualities we have enumerated, and there are others, *Les Tragiques* is not a complete success. There is too much exaggeration, too much partisanship, and perhaps simply too many lines. If the poem had been shorter, then its effect would have been more powerful and more gripping. By protracting his invective d'Aubigné sometimes allows his poetic style to suffer: the alexandrines become more prosaic than poetic, or he multiplies the alliterative effects to excess. There is too much of a tendency to hammer away with the big drum, whereas had he used more subtly all the instruments of the poetic orchestra the effect would have been more harmonious. The poem is, then, not without its defects, but it still deserves a much wider public than it has hitherto achieved. By replacing the work in its ideological and poetic context we can refute many of the criticisms of its so-called excesses. If the modern reader is prepared to put aside twentieth-century criteria for a while, then it will not be long before he will be caught up in the whirlwind invective and exciting narration of the heroic annals of Protestantism that constitute the essence of the epic poem, *Les Tragiques.*

CHAPTER 4

The Novelist

I   Les Avantures du Baron de Faeneste

AT the same time as d'Aubigné was engaged upon putting the final touches to his *Histoire universelle,* he took up his pen to attempt yet another literary genre, that of the novel. The idea behind *Les Avantures du Baron de Faeneste* was provided by an historical event. After Condé's disgrace in September, 1616, the inhabitants of La Rochelle, under the guidance of d'Aubigné, had occupied Rochefort and had thereby placed themselves in open conflict with the governor of the province, the duke of Epernon. The government in Paris wished to avoid a confrontation with the Protestants and wanted Epernon to come to terms with the Rochelois. After a cat and mouse sequence of events, including an alleged challenge to a duel from Epernon to d'Aubigné, a truce was negotiated leading eventually to peace in January, 1617. It is probable that d'Aubigné sought to ridicule Epernon in the character of Faeneste: both of them were of Gascon origin, both were burning with ambition, and both claimed to be of long noble descent. Furthermore, the "argument" of Book I of *Faeneste* informs us that the Baron was returning from the Aunis war.

The novel, published in 1617, comprised at first only two books,[1] a third being added in 1619, and the fourth, shortly before the author's death, in 1630. It is obvious that d'Aubigné was fond of this form of writing. The basic dialogue structure of the first two books was retained but the later volumes were much longer than the first two — the fourth book being three times as long as Book I, twice as long as Book II, and half as long again as Book III. Books II and IV contain more anecdotes and reveal a greater debt to the genre of the sixteenth-century *conte*. Their presentation, however, is less dynamic than in the first two books which form a compact unit of conversations.

In his preface, d'Aubigné suggests that he has turned to *Faeneste* as a means of recreation for his mind was weary of "discours graves et tragiques," an obvious reference to *Les Tragiques,* published in 1616 and to the *Histoire universelle,* which was to appear in 1618. He admits his intention of giving a description of his age by amassing "quelques bourdes vrayes." Such remarks are indicative of the author's wish to vary his literary output, as was always the case with this highly intelligent humanist. Not only in his youthful poetry but also in his most creative years, we find him composing a whole host of literary works which are linked by their theme and diversified by their form. The epic form of *Les Tragiques* is an emotional antithesis to the austerity and intended impartiality of the *Histoire universelle;* in its way, the *Faeneste* is another method of treating history. It constitutes an effort to comment upon contemporary events in a contemporary manner. By their close affinity with the comic theater, because of their dialogue form and their farcical elements, *Les Avantures du baron de Faeneste* portray their principal hero as being the "badin de la farce,"[2] a character caught up in the materialism of Marie de Medici's court, a victim, like the *capitaine fanfaron* of Italian and French Renaissance comedy, of his own ambition, his exaggerated idea of his own ability, and his own cowardice. Blind to his faults, he is following innocently the path of perdition. Such a picture contrasts strongly with the divine, tragic vision of the world as expounded in *Les Tragiques.* The *Histoire universelle, Les Tragiques,* and also *La Confession du sieur de Sancy,* all seek to explain the present in cosmic and in human terms: the *Faeneste* is a statement of what the present has produced. The link between the works is not only their author's view of history but also his constant desire for truth. At the end of the second book he echoes a remark in the preface by putting in the mouth of Enay the affirmation that: "Nous avons au commencement protesté de bourdes vrayes: nous n'avons rien dit en tout nostre discours qui ne soit arrivé, seulement avons nous attribué à un mesme ce qui appartient à plusieurs" (*F,* 726) ("At the beginning we spoke clearly of true 'deceits': we have said nothing in the whole of our discourse which has not happened, all we have done is to attribute to one person what belongs to several").

Such a claim to veracity is not uncommon among sixteenth-century *conteurs,* whether they be Rabelais or Marguerite de Navarre, but in the mouth of d'Aubigné it takes on a far greater significance. He was the avowed champion of truth, and *Faeneste* is dedicated to the task of unraveling truth from pretense. The principal theme of all four books is that of the primordial distinction to be made between appearance and reality, between "paraître" and "être."

This contrast is made evident right from the beginning of the book in the presentation of the two major characters, Faeneste and Enay. The former is a "Baron de Gascongne, Baron en l'air, qui a pour Seigneurie *Faeneste,* signifiant en Grec *paroistre;* cetui-là jeune éventé, demi courtisan, demi soldat"; and the latter, who resembles d'Aubigné himself, is described as "un vieil Gentilhomme nommé *Enay,* qui en mesme langue signifie *estre,* homme consommé aux lettres, aux experiences de la Cour et de la guerre" (*F,* preface). Not only do we find "paraître" opposed to "être," but also youth and inexperience to old age and wisdom. These two themes permeate the book and form the basis of most of the conversations.

II *The Presentation of the Story*

Throughout, Enay and Faeneste are the main interlocutors. They are joined only occasionally by Faeneste's servant, Cherbonnière, whose voice is necessary at times to provide an additional comic diversion, for he is able to reveal details which serve to ridicule the baron even more as he offers a realistic explanation of the baron's fantasies. In the fourth book, however, they are joined by the Sieur de Beaujeu, an army leader of the old school, who takes an active part in giving weight to Enay's contention that in the past things were very different from those at present. Apart from the *Argument* which precedes the first book and a few lines of presentation in the fourth, there is virtually no other source than dialogue for background and expository material. Each book begins with an encounter between the baron and Enay after a lapse of time. They begin their conversations where they discontinued them on a previous occasion and even at the end of Book IV there is a promise of a further meeting. H. Weber believes that this feature underlines the author's inability to conclude a work which finishes in true pamphlet fashion with a diatribe against contemporary corruption.[3] It is, however, a stylistic trait which had already been exploited by Rabelais in the saga of Pantagruel.

The Novelist

The use of dialogue was very widespread among d'Aubigné's precursors and contemporaries. It is a feature of the works of Rabelais and other *conteurs* such as Marguerite de Navarre, Noël du Fail, and Jacques Yver, not to mention the philosophical dialogues of the Socratic variety developed by Erasmus, Louis Le Caron, Henri Estienne, Jacques Tahureau, and others. Our author, perhaps in imitation of the comic dialogue of the theater, succeeds in reducing scenic and descriptive detail to an absolute minimum. The story, however, flows reasonably swiftly with short dynamic chapters.

Some of the subtleties involved cause the modern reader a certain difficulty, and although they are often of an historical nature, they are worth elucidating. The major obstacle is that of language. D'Aubigné has endeavored to parody the Gascon pronunciation of French in an overly systematized manner. For example, Faeneste pronounces *v*'s as *b*'s, as in these opening remarks:

Nous nous sommes esgarez dans un billage il y a une heure; car, pour bous dire, il m'est fashux de demander le chemin, et mes beilets de pieds sont demeurez arriere, hormis ce couquin trop gloriux pour parler à un bilen, s'il n'y en a dus. D'aillurs on ne peut faire marcher ce meschant relez: j'ai quitté à Surgeres mes roussens, en la compenio de Monsur de Cantelouz qui m'en aboit accommodé, ils sont miens et ne sont pas miens, on nous les garde pour une autre vegade. (*F,* 675)

An hour ago we lost our way in a village: for I must tell you that I find it annoying to ask the way, and my footmen have stayed behind, except for this rascal who is too proud to speak to a villain, unless there are two of them. Besides, we cannot get this wretched relay-horse to advance: I left my cob-horses in Surgères, in the company of Monsieur de Chanteloup who arranged it for me, they are mine and they are not mine, they are being kept for us for another time.

We should also point out other features: (*i*) *eu* becomes *u* (deux/dus, Monsieur/Monsur), *a* becomes *ei* (valet/beilet), *ain* and *in* are written *en* (vilain/bilen, roussin/roussen), *agnie* becomes *enio* (compagnie/compenio), and the author introduces words of Gascon origin such as *vegade* ("time"). Other vowels are deformed in the mouth of Faeneste, /ẓ/ is pronounced /j/ (courage/couraye), /ɔ/ becomes /u/ (colere/coulere). Such mispronunciations can lead to unfortunate incidents, as in Book III,

Chapter 13, where the confusion between "boire" and "voir" leads the baron to the brink of a duel. It could be argued that the constant use of such deformations has an overpowering effect and would confuse the reader of any age. On the other hand, it helps to make the character of Faeneste even more unique and to accentuate the satire of his Gascon bumptiousness. There can be no doubt that such a stylistic trait would have been more appreciated by d'Aubigné's own contemporaries, for they would have been able to recognize in Faeneste's language many of those pronunciations and expressions characteristic of those noblemen who had followed Henri IV to Paris and who had become enamored of court life and had burned with ambition.

III   *The Satirical Vein*

D'Aubigné seizes every opportunity to point the finger of ridicule at contemporary court custom, its attitudes toward war, women, magic, and religion. Enay is made to explain at the end of Book II that it is dangerous to take the "paraître" for the "être" in six things: "le gain, la volupté, l'amitié, l'honneur, le service du Roi ou de la Patrie, et la Religion." There is the obvious parallel between the character of Enay and d'Aubigné himself. Armand Garnier has shown how Enay's house recalls that of the Château de Mursay owned by the Huguenot author,[4] and the portrait the Baron gives of Enay in the closing pages of Book II confirms this supposition: "Tout lou monde bous connoist: bous avez de si vonnes places, tant fait de serbices; on bous a osté bos bieilles et noubelles pensions, bos garnisons n'ont esté paiees il y a dux ans, on bous pille, bous qui sauriez vien piller les autres, et bous ne boulez pas que nous parlions de l'Estat" (*F,* 727) ("Everyone knows you: you have such good strongholds, rendered so many services; they have taken away from you your old and new pensions, for two years your garrisons have not been paid, you are plundered, you who could very well plunder the others, and you do not want us to speak about the state"). The relationship between the two characters of Faeneste and Enay has been likened to that between Panurge and Pantagruel or Sancho Panza and Don Quixote[5] because of the antithesis in their natures of folly and wisdom. Faeneste is a poor match for Enay's insight, logic, and wisdom; he is constantly the object of satire, and yet, for all that, he remains a disarming, likeable personage. He is deceived by himself and by the world and has no foresight, no native intuition, nor any sense of personal ridiculousness.

The themes of satire introduced under the overriding opposition of "paraître"/"être" echo those of contemporary pamphlets. They are handled here with skill and their very presence highlights the author's austere Protestantism, his innate antipathy for deception and ostentation, and his hostility toward the regency court of Marie de Medici.

IV *The Courtier*

The foppish courtier of the regency incurs all of d'Aubigné's virulent wrath. Book I ends with a mordant sonnet denouncing the peacocklike qualities of the proud member of the court:

> Quand le Paon met au vent son pennache pompeux,
> Il s'admire soi-mesme et se tient pour estrange:
> Le Courtisan, ravi de sa vaine loüange,
> Voudroit comme le Paon estre parsemé d'yeux.
>
> Tous deux sont mal fondez; aussi de tous les deux,
> Quand il faut s'esprouver, la vaine gloire change,
> Comme le Paon miré dans son pennache d'Ange
> En desdaignant ses pieds devient moins glorieux.
>
> Encore est nostre Paon au Courtisan semblable,
> Que de la voix sans plus il se monstre effroiable:
> Il descouvre l'ami qui le loge chez lui,
>
> Il est jaloux de tout, il est subjet aux rheumes:
> Ils different d'un poinct, que l'un monstre ses plumes,
> Et que l'autre est paré du pennache d'autrui.
>
> (*F,* 696)

When the peacock airs his pompous plumage, he admires himself and considers himself to be out of the ordinary: the courtier, enraptured by his own vain praise, would like to be studded with eyes like the peacock.

Both of them are wrong; therefore, when they are put to the test, the vain glory of both of them changes, just as when the peacock, admired for his angelic plumage, becomes less proud when he looks at his feet with contempt.

Our peacock is again like the courtier, when he shows himself to be frightening by his voice and nothing more: he denounces the friend who houses him, he is jealous of everything, he is subject to colds: they differ on one point, in that one shows his own feathers, whereas the other is bedecked with someone else's plumage.

The courtier is only interested in appearances and public esteem: in other words, not his real value, but the value others are prepared to give him because of his position or fine manners. Faeneste entertained such desires, and through him we are introduced to the comic parody of contemporary dress which is all the more piquant because Faeneste is a "country bumpkin."[6] When he first meets Enay and notices that he is not wearing a ruff and a feathered hat, he almost takes him for a peasant. Faeneste himself never goes out without his sword, he is amply dressed according to the dictates of the latest fashion, bedecks himself with roses, and is particularly proud of his boots which he never leaves, for he follows the "trotte qui mode." So attached is he to his boots that the baron continues to use them even when he joins the infantry, thereby almost losing his life. This prompts Enay to riposte: "Peut estre apprendrez vous que l'estre vaut mieux que le parestre, pour le mal que vous avez receu à parestre botté" (*F,* 774) ("Perhaps you will learn that 'being' is better than 'appearing' because of the pain you received for appearing in boots'').

The courtier was just as ostentatious in his speech as in his dress. Faeneste constantly opposes his own terms to those of Enay — he wishes to call the domain around Enay's house a "parc" rather than a "clos," the drive an "allée" and not a "chemin," the house a "château" and not a "maison," etc. Enay, quoting "maistre Gervais," criticizes the courtiers for their exaggerated use of certain adverbs: "Tant de *Extremement, je suis vostre serviteur eternellement;* et aujourd'huy court *furieusement,* jusques à dire *il est sage, il est doux furieusement*" (*F,* 766) ("So many extremely's, I remain eternally your servant's; and today, what is current is, 'furiously,' even going so far as to say: he is furiously sensible or furiously sweet''). It is no surprise, then, when the baron appears at the beginning of Book IV, that he replies to Enay's greeting with a "Pour bous serbir eternellement" (*F,* 772), or that when he composes a love letter he mixes the courtly sublime with the ridiculous, finishing his missive with "nous bibons sayement, n'allant poent à la desbauche, prians Dieu, Madamiselle, qu'ainsi soit de bous" (*F,* 711). In fact, as must already be obvious, language plays an important part in d'Aubigné's satirical technique, for he highlights in an amusing manner the vanity and arbitrariness of certain forms of speech, thereby accentuating the comic separation that exists between words and fact.

V *Honor and Glory*

Like many others Faeneste is consumed by ambition: on arrival at court, after many farcical adventures in which he has been continually the dupe of those he met en route, he is introduced to the king's chamber and allowed to hold a candelabra for his majesty. With his back to a roaring fire the poor fellow is literally burned by ambition as his legs roast in the heat of the flames. The baron has a lofty, if twisted, sense of honor and hides his cowardice behind a front of bravura. Frequently, he is seen to extricate himself from a duel, the latter being a particular target of d'Aubigné's satire. Although banned by Henri IV, duelling was still tolerated and thousands of young noblemen lost their lives every year in the vain pretense of having no other means of keeping up the appearance of their honor. D'Aubigné, who had been in duels himself, is prepared to concede that in certain cases they may be justified:

Il y en a qui sont trés justes, assavoir quand le Roi les concede, ou pour crime de leze Majesté trop caché, ou pour accusation de trahison, ou pour maintenir l'honneur d'une femme de bien oppressee, ou pour supporter l'orfelin contre le meurtrier injuste du pere: encores, le combat de deux chefs entre leurs deux armees, pour espargner le sang d'une multitude: je mets à ce rang les duels qui se font pour la gloire du parti; il est vrai qu'il n'y en a qu'un des deux qui soit juste. (*F*, 691)

There are some which are very just, for example, when the king permits them, or for a too secret crime of lese-majesty, or for accusation of treason, or to safeguard the honor of an oppressed virtuous woman, or to support the orphan against the unworthy murderer of his father: or again, the combat of two leaders amid their two armies so as to spare the blood of the multitude: I put into this category the duels which are fought for the glory of the party; it is true that only one of the two is just.

His suggestion for suppressing duels is to cover the combattants in opprobrium rather than in glory. Faeneste often takes refuge behind a piercing question: "Où est l'honneur?" which on one occasion prompts Enay to relate an amusing anecdote to illustrate how honor can be debased. It concerns a certain Bribault who, because Henri IV had taunted him with "Où est l'honneur? Si vous en avez, vous ferez ce que je commande" (*F,* 724), took the king's place in the bed of an old "maquerelle" who quickly discovered the subterfuge and subjected Bribault to a ridiculous plight. This story full of piquancy must have pleased d'Aubigné who had refused to serve as an intermediary in the king's amorous pursuits.[7]

Linked to the theme of honor, which in the case of many is more a desire to "paraître" than "être," is that of glory. In the fourth book the topic is developed by Enay and he makes the distinction between three types of glory: the divine, about which nothing can be said in their conversations; the cavalier's, which consists in "parcere subjectis et debellare superbos"; and finally the barber's, which is all show, "gist en morgues, ou en affetterie de putain, en habits à la mode, et telles marchandises" (*F,* 779). As one would expect, Faeneste and the courtiers belong to the last category. The satire is however not just aimed at a particular group of individuals; its implications are far more widespread. Beaujeu introduces the story of another type of glory, the "glori Bernat," revealed by the tale of the old man forced to dress up for his son's wedding and is consequently so trussed up in unfamiliar clothes that he disgraces himself by not being able to undo his hose in time to relieve himself. The terms of reference are constantly extended and in the ensuing chapter the "morgue," the pride of a Spaniard, is mocked as the others present eat his portion of chicken while he is rolling off his string of names; elsewhere, the subject of ridicule is a Bordeaux counselor hoaxed into believing that he has been appointed chancellor to the king of Portugal. Such anecdotes stress d'Aubigné's comic vision of a world full of vanity and self-delusion. The author knows how to create a comic situation and in the tradition of comedy his characters become victims of their own vices. Games are described in which the baron appears ridiculous because of his failure to understand that others have tricked him — the absence of any awareness of ridiculousness is essential for a good comic personage.

VI *Love and the Occult*

In his love adventures, Faeneste reveals weaknesses which were shared by many of his contemporaries. Set against the background of the regency court dominated by the Concinis who dabbled in black magic, Faeneste's practices follow a familiar pattern. He has been gullibly trapped into having recourse to enchantments and magic to further his venial aims; and Enay's reaction to the methods employed to foresee the future and to conjure up the image of the beloved reveal the same common sense and skepticism shown sixty years later by Thomas Corneille and Donneau de Visé in their play, *La Devineresse* (1680), which was based on the *Affaire des Poisons.*

Palma Cayet, a minister at Henri's court and a former Huguenot, is savagely accused by Enay of having given himself to the Devil "par cédule signee de sa main, stipulee de la main de l'acquereur" (*F,* 714). Faeneste is too enamored of the facile aspects of life at Court — "ostez en les Dames, les duels et les balets, ye ne voudrois pas bibvre" (*F,* 721) — not to be attracted by the occult arts and all this in spite of an unfortunate experience. Having met a magician, Saint-Felix, who, so he claimed, possessed the ability to make a man invisible, the credulous Faeneste allowed himself to be led around "disguised" as a horse, a lion, a donkey, and a stool! (*F,* 722). It is obvious that the people to whom Faeneste was introduced in such a form were aware of the subterfuge involved. The most grotesque situation arises when Faeneste, attending a gathering, is told by those present that he is naked. Saint-Felix explains that were he to appear naked then the others would think he were clothed — Faeneste followed his counsel and the reader can imagine the hilarious, if disastrous, consequences that ensue. The episode is dismissed by Enay, however, with the mordant remark: "Tous magiciens sont sujets à faire des fautes, car le Diable est trompeur" (*F,* 723).

VII *The Confidence Tricksters*

The debunking of magicians by Enay is linked with the attitude adopted toward confidence tricksters in the novel. Enay sees through the Comte de Lorme who has come to court offering untold wealth to Concini (*F,* 755), and he suggests that he is a penniless imposter. Similarly, the anecdote of the Theologal of Maillezais stresses the gullibility of others, for the poor man was convinced by a gypsy that a spell had been cast upon him. While he was at her house trying to break the spell the other gypsies burgled his own abode. When Cherbonnière goes on to describe other exploits, Enay is highly amused, thereby suggesting that the appeal of the "astuce" was great for d'Aubigné. In the tradition of the sixteenth-century *conteurs,* finesse is seen as an admirable quality when used to punish the gullible and the haughty. The technique is frequently used to ridicule the baron, for he is far too much concerned with "paraître." In his manner of walking he follows that of the courtiers, with "un peu de grabitai, trainant une jamve à la cadence de la teste, comme font tous les galands hommes" (*F,* 716). He bases his nobility on the most fragile of antecedents. His ancestors had had noble treatment: for example, his grandfather was beheaded at Toulouse for having raped a nun, and the same fate befell his uncle and nephew for having killed a priest. Through such remarks by Faeneste, d'Aubigné attacks the emptiness of the courtier with all his naive pretensions and futile actions.[8] This opposition to the flattering and fawning courtier had already been adumbrated in *Princes:*

> Quand ce siecle n'est rien qu'une histoire tragique,
> Ce ne sont farces et jeux toutes leurs actions;
> Un ris sardonien peint leurs affections,
> Bizarr' habits et coeurs, les plaisants se desguisent....
> (T, II, ll.206-9)

When this century is nothing but a tragic story, all their acts are merely farces and plays; a sardonic laugh covers their feelings; in strange clothes and hearts, the jokers disguise themselves.

Such sentiments as these color the portrait of the baron; but on the other hand, the attitude adopted by d'Aubigné in the *Faeneste* (to this aspect of the human condition) is a more humane and understanding one.[9]

VIII *Military Practices*

Faeneste considers himself a soldier of some prowess, yet it is evident that he talks more than he acts. When we first meet him he is returning from the Aunis war, the confrontation between the duke of Epernon and the Rochelois at Rochefort. We learn too that he had already been in three other "wars," Savoy in 1600, Juliers in 1610, and the prince of Condé's uprising in 1615-1616. Like the

The Novelist 93

Capitaine Fanfaron of sixteenth-century comedy, he is a boaster; as Cherbonnière says, "quand il trouve des gens qui l'escoutent à gueule bee, vous ne sçauriez croire ce qu'il dit" (*F,* 735). In spite of his claims, when in actual danger he talks his way out of it in a cowardly fashion (*F,* 740). The most consistent treatment of the war theme is to be found in Book IV where Beaujeu makes pointed comparisons between contemporary military techniques and those of his own day. The baron confesses to have been in three encounters, at the Pont de Cé in 1620, the Valtellina Pass in 1625, and St. Pierre in 1628. He had changed from the cavalry to the infantry for a typical reason: "comme le seul moyen de parestre et de parbenir" (*F,* 772). An example of Faeneste's desire to "paraître" is his persistent use of boots even when an infantryman. This, along with pillaging, is one of the criticisms leveled by Beaujeu at the conduct of this branch of the army. All Faeneste's exploits ended in disaster, and through him not only the contemporary soldier is attacked, but also his incompetent commanders.[10] One can but appreciate the irony of Enay's closing statement that "Vrayement, Monsier le Baron, vous nous avez conté des combats si estranges, que l'Antiquité n'en a guaires de pareils" (*F,* 818).

IX *Religion*

As is to be expected, there is a strong religious current running through the pages of *Faeneste*. This theme is developed at some length in the second and subsequent books. When the topic of religion is introduced in Book I, Enay dismisses it quickly; for although he says of the Christian, "il faut l'estre pour le paroistre" (*F,* 692), he adds, "Mais, s'il vous plaist, nous ne ferons pas de la Theologie un propos de table." Nonetheless, various aspects of Catholicism receive a broadside from d'Aubigné's satirical guns. He ridicules Faeneste's practices, his use of Latin graces which only refer to the Virgin and not to Christ (*F,* 697), the lack of conviction in so-called Huguenot converts to Catholicism (*F,* 699), the opposition between the invisible Huguenot God and the vain attempts of the Catholics to make theirs visible. This is seen, he claims, in the widespread use of relics (*F,* 700), the contemporary controversy over the priest's intention and the value of the sacrament, the latter depending upon the former (*F,* 701), false miracles and arranged diabolic exorcisms (*F,* 704–706), the problem of the existence of limbo (*F,* 708-710), Catholic trickery to give credence to pilgrimages (*F,* 736), immorality of members of Catholic religious orders (*F,* 801): and the "paraître" of Catholicism is contrasted with the "être" of Protestantism in a masterly parody of a Catholic sermon (*F,* 793) given by Père Ange, which is preceded by the portrait of a precursor of the vicar of Bray, the Curé d'Eschilais, who changed religions to suit his own advantage (*F,* 791). The sermon of Père Ange is reminiscent of the fifteenth-century sermons of the Franciscan Olivier Maillard; it is permeated with a great deal of histrionics — the opening lines being: "Nouvelles, nouvelles nouvelles!... (là une grande pause). Et quelles nouvelles?... (là encore une), de querelles, de guerres entre de grands Seigneurs" (*F,* 793). It proceeds to describe in dramatic terms the struggle between Christ and the devil, the imagery being that of a colloquial account of a contemporary battle. Christ is credited with a language which is disrespectful and even blasphemous, the preacher being concerned with effect rather than truth. For example:

"quand Sathan le conviant à se jetter du pinacle en bas, il respondit, *como Cavallero bien criado: Beso las manos, Señor Sathanas, por que yo tengo escalas para bajarme.* Lui donc, estant encor esmeu de la charge qu'il venoit de faire, Sathan s'approcha en colere aussi, et fort resolument lui dit: "Je te maintiens que tu n'es point le fils de Dieu. — Tu en as menti (dit le Seigneur) par ta puante gorge, ce que je te maintiendrai à telles armes que tu voudras." (*F,* 794)

When Satan invited him to throw himself down from the peak to the bottom, he replied, *Como Cavallero bien criado: Beso las manos, Señor Sathanas, por que yo tengo escalas para bajarme.* [As a well brought up gentleman, I take my leave of you, Satan, sir, for I have ladders whereby to descend.] While he was then still moved by the onslaught he had just made, Satan came closer and in anger and with great resolution, said to him: "I maintain that you are not the son of God. You, said the Lord, have lied with your stinking mouth, and I shall maintain that by any weapons you like."

Père Ange is made to foresee eventual Protestant criticism, for he then adds: "Ces propos, au jugement des Ministres, seroient des blasphemes, mais nous autres appellons le pain, pain, et disons les choses comme elles sont; tant y a que Sathan le prend au mot, demande à loisir l'election des armes" (*F,* 794) ("In the view of your ministers, these remarks would be blasphemous, but, we

The Novelist 95

others, we call bread bread and say things as they are; the fact remains that Satan took him at his word, and at leisure asks for a choice of weapons"). The whole sermon is a masterpiece of sustained satire and it is indicative of its intended seriousness as a parody that Enay is depicted as becoming unusually heated when the baron attempts to interrupt Beaujeu's narration, even going so far at one stage as to exclaim: "Taisez-vous, si vous pouvez" (*F,* 796). The sermon ends on a farcical note, as the preacher, to convey the force of the death of Christ, pulls a noose from his pocket, places it around his neck, and mimics Christ's end. The reaction of the congregation reveals all d'Aubigné's bitter irony and no doubt heartfelt disgust at such behavior: "Toute la voute retentissoit de cris des spectateurs, qui avoient changé les ris en plaintes, l'entrée comique en tragedie, laquelle fut toutefois sacrifice non sanglant" (*F,* 797) ("The whole vault resounded with the shouts of the congregation, who changed their laughter into lamentations, the comic beginning into the tragic, which was not, however, a bloody sacrifice").

As we shall see, a number of these traits had already been satirized in the *Confession du Sieur de Sancy,* and from the point of view of religious satire the two works complement one another, *Faeneste* being more oblique in its approach than the *Sancy,* which by its form belongs to the genre of the pamphlet.

X Politics

The latent opposition to the ruling class, to the attitudes prevalent at court, toward the army and religion has been obvious in our previous analysis of *Faeneste*. It reaches its climax in the closing pages of Book IV when the work introduces the satirical element reminiscent of the pamphlet in the form of caricature with the *Triomphes*. Inspired by the *Satire Ménippée,* which had been such a successful weapon in 1594 in combatting the League by the use of ridicule, d'Aubigné imagines Madame La Varenne whose husband had risen from his humble origins as cook to the elevated rank of "contrôleur général des postes," ordering some tapestries from Lyons to decorate her château, beginning naturally with the kitchen! He then proceeds to a description of the four sets of tapestries which in opposition to Petrarch's triumph of Chastity, represent the triumph of Impiety, Ignorance, Cowardice, and Mendicity (*F,* 820–30). In this set of grotesque descriptions d'Aubigné calls upon his evocative powers of personifying abstract qualities and vices, a talent of which he had already made use in *La Chambre dorée,* in *Les Tragiques.*

There is a certain similarity in the way each of the tapestry sets is presented: a description is given of the animals leading the triumphal chariot, the vice itself with her attendants, and then the prisoners with their taskmasters. The prisoners in all except the third set of tapestries are divided into three groups representative of the historical divisions to be found in *Vengeances,* the first being devoted to personages from the Old Testament, the second to those of the early church and the third to the contemporary period. Great attention is paid to the telling physical details of the vices — Impiety, for example, is on a chariot drawn by four "grands vilains beaux Diables."

Sur la place de derrier, plus haute que les autres (comme il appartient à celle du triomphant), estoit un monstre en forme de vieille femme fardee, comme le visage de Perrette quand elle avoit gagné les pardons. Elle avoit tout d'humain pourtant, horsmis qu'il lui estoit impossible de lever la face en haut, mais l'avoit ployée en terre comme les brutes; les oreilles lui pendoient comme à un bracque, et la faisoient sourde par leur espesseur. Vous luy voyez les yeux petits, comme les avoit Madame de Mersec, quand elle crioit à la S. Barthelemi: *Achevez tout!* (F, 820–21)

On the seat at the rear, higher than the others (as befits that of the person in a triumph) was a monster in the form of an old made-up woman, like Perrette's face when she had won the pardons. However, she looked perfectly human, except she could not lift her face up but had it cast down like that of idiots; the ears were hanging down like those of a hound and made her deaf because of their thickness. You can see she has little eyes, like Madame de Mersec had when she was shrieking on St. Bartholomew's Day: Kill everything!

Such descriptions reveal the intention of d'Aubigné to draw a strict parallel between the figures in the triumphs and his contemporaries. Impiety is attended by Voluptuousness, Conscience, and Stupidity — the first group of prisoners comprises the patriarchs and saints of the Old Testament under the domination of Cain, Nembroth, Pharoah, and others. They walk upon the broken tables of the Mosaic Law and the Covenant. Following these are the apostles, martyrs, and confessors of the early church, maltreated by Nero, Domitian, Hadrian, and others down to Julian the Apostate, the latter bearing a resemblance to one of d'Aubigné's contemporaries, and Libanius too looked very much like the Cardinal du Perron; finally, the modern martyrs of the faith are portrayed under the oppression of the Inquisition. Ignorance, in a carriage drawn by four donkeys, is a naked lady reading a breviary which obviously gives her great enjoyment — her handmaidens are Folly, Stubbornness, and Superstition, bedecked with rosaries. The captives in the first band are Noah, Moses, the prophets ill at ease under the powerful hands of the Giants and rebellious Jews. The doctors of the early church are subjected to the cruelties of the Pope Liberius and the victorious Arians — the contemporary victims are the German doctors who preached against drunkenness, Calvin, the twelve ministers of Poissy, Roche-Chandieu's sisters, Du Plessis-Mornay, forced to trample over such books as Calvin's *Institution chrétienne,* Du Plessis-Mornay's *Mystère d'iniquité,* Du Bartas' *La Sepmaine,* and d'Aubigné's *Histoire Universelle,* under the stern eye of Lignerac, Birague, Menot the preacher, Cayet, Father Cotton, etc.

These first two triumphs thus resume the satirical tendencies in *Faeneste.* In criticizing contemporary attitudes toward religion they also recall not only the *Confession du Sieur de Sancy* and *Les Tragiques,* but the whole of d'Aubigné's venom and vituperation which he expressed in outrage at what he thought was the suppression of truth and injustice toward the true faith.

The remaining sets of tapestries are concerned more with the other theme of *Faeneste,* namely, the materialism of the court. Cowardice in a chariot drawn by four deer and four foxes, ("on dit qu'elle a fait ses affaires dans ses chausses" [*F,* 825]), is surrounded by Comfort, Laziness, and Shame. The other tapestries do not give an example of cowardice from the Old Testament or antiquity because this vice belongs only to modern times. Those who are there, under the domination of Marshal de Retz, the Sieur de Lansac, d'O, and others guilty of cowardice, are the brave men from the troops of the Bourbons, Lorraine, the Châtillons, the battle of the St. Barthélemy, etc. The procession is depicted against a backcloth of houses under the sign of the law courts and the emblem, "Dispari Domino Dominaris," revealing d'Aubigné's lament at the disappearance of Justice.

The descriptions come to a close with that of Mendicity whose chariot, like that of her predecessors, is drawn by animals. This time it is by four lean she wolves, in the company of Insolence, Debauchery, and Flattery. The next tapestry shows exiled kings, and then another is devoted to those Romans such as Seneca, Helvidius Priscus, and Thrasea who espoused the cause of liberty. The modern scene is one dear to d'Aubigné's own heart: it is that of the ungrateful treatment meted out by kings to those who have served them well. Their reward is contrasted with the exaltation of the members of the Catholic church, the *parvenus,* but those who have earned their nobility through their achievement are banished from the triumph. As it passes, Mendicity's chariot smashes heraldic shields and signs and even that of the Fleurs de Lys. We can be certain that d'Aubigné, remembering his own treatment at the hands of the queen regent and Louis XIII, agreed, in his pride as a Huguenot and faithful soldier, with the remarks he places in Beaujeu's mouth that: "En fin, c'est une Prophetie en tapisserie, qui promet aux traistres, aux bestes, aux poltrons et aux belistres les gouvernements, les Estats, les honneurs et les biens, tant que les gens de bien, les doctes, les braves et les Grands auront agreable de perir par honnesteté (*F,* 830) ("In a word, it is a prophecy in tapestry, which promises to the traitors, the idiots, the cowards, and the unscrupulous, the governorships, the states, the honors and wealth, so that the good people, the learned, the courageous, and the mighty will be pleased to perish by honesty").

It is in these closing pages that we come face to face once more with the tremendous visual quality of d'Aubigné's writing. As we saw in *Les Tragiques,* the keystone to the tableaulike structure of the work was d'Aubigné's vision — his method of composition is to a great extent governed by his being able to imagine a scene. In the same way that in formulary rhetoric the student had to imagine what a person would say and how he would react in given circumstances, so we have d'Aubigné asking himself how such and such a scene could be represented. His mind's eye sees quite literally the tableaux depicted in tapestry form, and he summons up all his art to make the pictures as horrifying and as mordant as possible. A further example of such a tendency is to be found also in the fourth book again when Beaujeu describes the painting, the "Grotesque de la Terne" (*F,* 807) which is modeled on the procession of the League.[11]

The Novelist

XI Structure of Faeneste

Faeneste is composed totally of dialogue, the story progressing through the use of direct and reported speech. This technique gives the work a certain dynamism and dramatic quality. The third and fourth books introduce more diversity into the exchanges between Enay and Faeneste, and this is through the increasing use of the exemplary *conte*. In the third book Cherbonnière and Enay discuss the life of the Dame de la Coste thereby providing Enay's countersally of the incident of the Theologal of Maillezais (*F,* 729-33). In fact, the two interlocutors continue for some time in this vein of exchanging narrations, many of which would not have been a discredit to Rabelais. The one concerning the pride and subterfuge of the doctor, Beaumier, is obviously modeled on Rabelais' anecdote of Jean Tappecou in the *Quart Livre* (Chapter XIII) and d'Aubigné himself recalls "Maître François" (*F,* 738).[12] Similarly, Faeneste's dream (*F,* 739) is reminiscent of that of Panurge in the *Tiers Livre* (Chapter XIV). The same book also contains the enigma of the *filasse* (F, 746-53) which can be likened to that of the description of Pantagruélion at the end of the *Tiers Livre* and the enigma in the last chapter of *Gargantua*. Like the enigma found in the foundations of the Abbaye de Thélème, the one given to Faeneste was "une prouphetie troubee aux mines de Partenai lou Biux" (*F,* 747). It is evident that one of the interpretations of the enigma is a presage of disaster and political upheaval. The fact that it is read by Enay and not by Faeneste guarantees it maximum comprehensibility. Enay's interpretation is the innocuous, humorous one of the enigma referring to tow and to the difficulties involved in its cultivation; it is another satirical thrust in keeping with the theme of the novel, that of "paraître" and "être." Although the original idea may have been provided by his reading of Rabelais, d'Aubigné adapts it to his own requirements. In the same way, when he describes Faeneste's games, we can find the prototype in *Gargantua* and in *Pantagruel,* where the young Gargantua or Panurge have the upper hand. Yet in *Faeneste* the games are used to illustrate his stupidity and blindness to what is going on (see *F,* 702-704). There can be no doubt that the reading of Rabelais left a profound impression on our author. Jacques Bailbé has drawn the parallel between Pantagruel's navigation and the story of the Baron de Calopse which is developed at length in the third book of *Faeneste* (*F,* 763-71). They can be likened too to those of Don Quixote. The Baron de Calopse undertakes his journey to discover why "l'Estat alloit mal, et du remede qui s'y pourroit trouver" (F, 765). The journey is farcical and the events even more so.

There is a strong *conteur* flavor to the fourth book with the introduction of the parodied sermons and the scurrilous details of the cloistered life. Generally speaking, the link between the chapters is well maintained,[13] and often a theme just touched upon in one book is treated fully in a subsequent one. Against the general antithetical opposition of "paraître" and "être," it is possible to single out a dominant theme in each book. Book I deals with the court, Book II with religion and the occult, Book III with confidence tricksters and the use of cunning, and Book IV with war and the vain pursuit of glory.

XII *Style*

D'Aubigné shows a masterly use of language in *Faeneste*.[14] He employs many Rabelaisian techniques of making a *récit* come alive — puns and patois are constantly interwoven into the fabric of the text and reveal the author's own taste for this somewhat sophisticated form of writing. Their use is however not gratuitous and when d'Aubigné provides a speech in dialect form it is to bring out the essential truth to be found in the simplicity of the expression, as for example in the discussion about the existence of limbo between Clochard and Mathé in Book II, Chapter IX. As Henri Weber has pointed out,[15] there is a repeated mechanism in the employment of tales and details opposing "paraître" and "être," and this is the opposition of words to things. Faeneste has a word to describe his actions such as "l'honneur," but when the description is confronted with the action, then we see not only a comic juxtaposition of the two but the Baron's own folly in mistaking appearance for reality.

Great exploitation is made of the Baron's ingenuousness. This man who has spent twenty thousand nights on horseback has never seen the sun on its way back to its position for sunrise, and he does not understand how it passes beneath the ground! (F, 739). For the most part the humorous device preferred by d'Aubigné is that of irony and he does not produce the belly laugh of a Rabelais.[16]

Incorporated into the text are a number of verse satires directed against d'Aubigné's contemporaries. One such satire, of his own composition, "Le Paon," closes the first book; elsewhere Enay quotes epigrammatic lines which are reminiscent of the most vicious of Huguenot attacks (see *F,* 705-6, 715, 726, 764); on other occasions Faeneste reiterates current doggerel (*F,* 753-55), as does Beaujeu (*F,* 803). These stylistic features which belong to the "style bas" could surprise us in the mouth of such an austere personage as Enay. To them, we could add some of the lascivious tales of the third and fourth books. Yet to understand their impact it is necessary to replace them in the historical context of the *conte* tradition and Huguenot satire. This same juxtaposition of the refined and the crude also existed in d'Aubigné's literary production when seen as a whole, for it not only includes works of the highest piety but also betrays something of the earthy soldier, of the whole sixteenth-century man. In the *Faeneste* there is a trace of Agrippa d'Aubigné not only in Enay but also in the baron and Beaujeu. As Rocheblave has written: "Nothing is more intolerable to intelligent men than to see their defects and even their qualities exaggerated and deformed by a neighbor. It is but a short step then to hate and to ridicule the traitor."[17]

It is a feature of sixteenth-century satire, as of that of many another age, that to attack those in authority it is most expedient to attack them on moral grounds. This is transparent when one reads *Les Tragiques,* where the criminal protagonists are accused frequently of the most heinous sexual misdemeanors. Such practices were echoed by d'Aubigné's own contemporaries, whether they were Protestant or Catholic. We must not overlook either that the "style bas" was also an integral part of comedy and of the "roman burlesque." Jacques Bailbé has recently shown that *Faeneste* owes much to the "style burlesque."[18] This is evident not only from the use of certain themes, as in Books III and IV where parody and caricature play an important role, but also at the purely stylistic level, where d'Aubigné shows his skill at producing "fantaisie verbale" by using surprise and dissonance, enumeration, burlesque narrations, etc. The author has not espoused, however, a world of complete fantasy but has based his narration on a real satirical view of contemporary society.

By adopting the form he did for *Faeneste,* d'Aubigné appears to have been trying to take advantage of the current interest in the Spanish picaresque novels which were becoming increasingly popular in the second decade of the seventeenth century. The political rapprochement between France and Spain by the double marriage in 1615 of Louis XIII with Anne of Austria, and of Elizabeth of Bourbon, his sister, with the future Philip IV, stimulated the introduction of Spanish customs and fashions into France.[19] Cervantes was beginning to make his mark on French literature and in 1611 F. de Rosset and D'Audiguier published a translation of the *Novales Exemplares,* just a year after their appearance in Spain. This was followed in 1618 by the publication of the two parts of *Don Quixote* translated by Cesar Oudin.[20] The following lines taken from the *Au lecteur* of Jean Chapelain's translation of *Le Gueux ou La Vie de Guzman d'Alfarache,* published in Paris in 1621, could well be applied to the *Faeneste:* "What is excellent in him is the exact description of society's malpractices, how people live now in all walks of life, the details of which he examines with such knowledge and clarity that we can desire nothing more; the tales are hardly ever tales, and digression is a license he uses and with prudence; for it is there that lies the benefit of reading him."

It is important to add Reynier's reservations that the character of Faeneste had been so exaggerated as to be out of touch with the reality of the period and that he belongs more to the tradition of the "miles gloriosus."[21] And yet, how justified is this objection? Although it is true that both Faeneste and Enay have a large number of symbolic attributes and have a contrastive role, it cannot be denied that d'Aubigné has endeavored to replace them in a satirical context which gives them life, if not credibility. The wealth of contemporary allusions makes the object of satire very tangible and criticisms made by d'Aubigné of the contemporary scene fit in very well with those of other authors of the period.

Faeneste is a work which withstands frequent reading. A cursory perusal of it reveals a text fraught with difficulties of comprehension not only on the linguistic level but also in the determination of the satirical objective. Once these problems have been ironed out, we realize that d'Aubigné has produced a book which marks an important point in the transition of the novel from the sixteenth-century collection of *contes* to the literature of the seventeenth and eighteenth centuries, in which the exploration of character and social satire were increasingly exploited.

XIII Fortune of Faeneste

It has been suggested that the scandal which erupted at the appearance of the fourth book and thus the complete edition of *Faeneste* in Geneva in 1630 may have hastened the death of its author.[22] The printer Pierre Aubert was summoned to appear before the "Petit Conseil" in Geneva on March 29, 1630, for having published without permission the *Baron de Faeneste,* a book containing "plusieurs choses impies et blasphématoires qui scandalisent les gens de bien."[23] He was sentenced to imprisonment, later given a fine of one hundred écus, and made to retrieve and destroy all the copies of the book. D'Aubigné himself was summoned to appear before the Scholarques to be admonished for having written such a work, and to promise that "désormais il se déporte de faire semblables escrits lesquels ne peuvent qu'apporter du mal à cest Estat."[24] His subsequent death assured that his promise was binding!

All copies of *Faeneste* were clearly not destroyed, but they became difficult to find. One has to wait another century before Le Duchat's annotated edition of the book appeared.[25] In his preface to the work, the eighteenth-century editor recounts how thirty years previously he had heard from an inhabitant of Dijon that the Great Condé had had considerable trouble in finding a copy of this "Satire si ingenieuse, mais en même temps si enveloppée pour les lecteurs de ce temps."[26] In the nineteenth century, before the Réaume edition, Prosper Mérimée refound *Faeneste* and republished "this most outstanding tableau of manners, and if we strip it of the exaggerations that accompany this type of satire, it offers a lively and faithful picture of the society at the time the author lived. But what appears especially admirable in these dialogues is the truth of the characters portrayed and the rare talent for observation which is to be found right down to the smallest detail."[27] We feel that we can still concur with such a view.

Since Mérimée and Réaume *Faeneste* has attracted only sporadically the attention of scholars. More recently, however, a number of articles devoted to this work have appeared, as revealed by our footnotes. Let us express our pious hope that this attention of scholars will succeed in making the *Faeneste* more widely known and thus allow this minor masterpiece of the early seventeenth century to be appreciated for its just merits.

CHAPTER 5

The Satirist

I Confession Catholique du Sieur de Sancy

LIKE so many other works of d'Aubigné, the *Catholic Confession of the Lord of Sancy*[1] was only published years after his death. It appeared in 1660 in the *Recueil de diverses pièces servant à l'Histoire de Henri III* and was republished several times during the seventeenth and eighteenth centuries. Its inclusion in such a collection reveals the tone of the work: it reflects upon the character of Nicolas Harlay de Sancy (1546–1629) as well as upon the reigns of Henry III and Henry IV. It is a parody of a confession and belongs to the genre of the pamphlet, of which there were many during the last ten years of Henry III's reign and throughout that of Henry IV and the Regency period.

Sancy was brought up as a Protestant and became a Catholic in Orléans in 1572 to escape the massacre which followed in the provinces the St. Bartholomew's Day murders in Paris. Shortly afterward he embraced the Protestant faith again, but this did not prevent his rise to power under Henry III: he became successively a counselor at the parlement in Paris, "maître des requêtes," and then a privy counselor. He raised money for Swiss mercenaries. Under Henry IV he was appointed to the important post of superintendent of finances in 1594, and in 1596 he was sent as ambassador to Elizabeth I of England. In that same year he became the colonel-in-chief of the Swiss Guards. The following year he decided to espouse Catholicism, an action which it is reputed solicited from Henry IV the remark that "all his superintendent now needed was to take the turban by becoming a Muslim."[2] This third conversion did not have the effect Sancy desired for, instead of increasing in royal favor, he lost it, mainly because of the antipathy the king's mistress, Gabrielle d'Estrées, had for him. As a result, he was replaced as superintendent of finances in 1599 by Sully, and he went into retirement in 1605.

Although Sancy in the *Confession* is depicted before his final disgrace, d'Aubigné foresaw such a fate as a fitting recompense for a life of falsehood. For him, Sancy represented many French noblemen who had changed their religion in the hope of material gain. Such a theme was also linked in his mind with the way in which the Huguenot cause had been betrayed by members of its own party. He was also disturbed at the apparent success of one of the main Catholic spokesmen, Jacques Davy du Perron (1556–1618), who, in November, 1593, had defended successfully the king's abjuration against the Huguenot, Rotan, at the Protestant Assembly at Mantes. Rotan, according to d'Aubigné, had sabotaged the Huguenot cause (see *C,* 639). Du Perron had developed into the main Catholic opponent of the Huguenots. He was well equipped for such a role, as his father had been a Calvinist minister. As a child he was raised in Switzerland where, like d'Aubigné, he became expert in Latin, Greek, Hebrew, mathematics, and philosophy. He earned the protection of the court poet Philippe Desportes and after embracing Catholicism, he became a "lecteur royal" to Henry III and entered holy orders. A careful and intelligent man, he was the confidant of the aged Cardinal de Bourbon and also managed to enjoy the favor and support of Henry IV. In 1591, he was appointed bishop of Evreux and was instrumental in the conversion of the king. It was he who converted Jean de Sponde and Sancy; thus d'Aubigné refers to him as "le grand convertisseur." On May 4, 1600, he represented victoriously the Catholic church in the disputation held at Fontainebleau against Du Plessis-Mornay, spokesman for the Huguenots. D'Aubigné was of the view that Du Plessis-Mornay had been unfairly treated, and therefore he felt even more antagonistic toward du Perron. As a reward for his services du Perron was created a cardinal in 1604. It was to ridicule the arguments of du Perron and to illustrate the materialist reasons that incited Huguenots of weak faith to abjure, that d'Aubigné undertook the composition of his mordant satire.

II *Content*

The work is written as a parody of a confession of a convert to Catholicism, of which a number had been published in the 1590s, such as the *Déclaration des principaux motifs qui induisirent le Sr de Sponde à s'unir à l'Eglise C.A. et R.* (1593). Sponde himself is often mentioned in derogatory terms in the *Sancy*. The charm of the parody comes from the ironic naiveté of Sancy himself. The remainder of the title of the book is very reminiscent of Sponde's "Et declaration des causes, tant d'estat que de religion, qui l'ont meu à se remettre au giron de l'eglise romaine." As this clearly indicates, Sancy's apology contains references to the political and religious forces which not only influenced him but were at work throughout the kingdom. The book is dedicated to du Perron as bishop of Evreux, and the dedication parodies the genre in the way Sancy explains why he has chosen as the dedicatee, "Monsieur [son] Convertisseur." Du Perron's skill, it is suggested, lies in defending seemingly heretical points, such as the validity of the Koran and the Talmud, or the proposition that God does not exist, or that homosexuality is not to be condemned, etc. Although this may be a tribute to his eloquence, it is certainly a pointed attack against the bishop's own orthodoxy. Sancy also refers to apostate Huguenots such as Sponde and Cayet, and finishes on a reaffirmation of his faith in the bishop and his teaching, swearing to follow his advice "objective et subjective ... jusques à une heure devant la mort" (*C*, 577).

The disarmingly naive note continues and Sancy, revealing his lack of discrimination, examines a whole host of topics in the first ten chapters of the first book — the relative position of church and state, the role of the pope, the tradition of the Catholic church, the intercession of the saints, the concept of purgatory, good works, miracles, relics, vows, conversions, transubstantiation — topics which reveal d'Aubigné's wide knowledge of contemporary events and controversies.

The second book begins with a lively exchange between Mathurine, the "folle," a member of Henry IV's court, and Jean Davy (1565-1621), brother of the cardinal, who succeeded his brother as archbishop of Sens. In 1614, he published an *Apologie pour les Jésuites,* and he was often present with his brother at theological assemblies. The dialogue has a sparkling freshness and dynamism and although it contains several "low" references, it is a witty satire of court manners, supremely preferable to many contemporary pamphlets. There are references on this occasion to another conversion to Catholicism, that of Robert, baron of Sainte

The Satirist

Marie du Mont, who was converted by Mathurine around 1600 with sexual — or so it is suggested — rather than with spiritual arguments.

The remaining eight chapters of the second book deal with various aspects of the religious problem, permitting d'Aubigné to vent his criticisms through the mouth of Sancy — on the moves to find a common ground for the unity of the two religions, on the details of Sancy's second conversion to Catholicism, and his reasons for having remained a Huguenot for so long, his disdain of Huguenot poverty, his interest lying only in "le profit, l'honneur, l'aise et la seurté" (*C*, 641). He goes through some of the books used to convert people to Catholicism, attacks the Huguenots for their outspoken criticism of the country's leaders and their faith. There follows a list of martyrs for the Catholic faith, pouring scorn on them and thus illustrating indirectly the purity of the Protestant martyrs, as seen in Jean Crespin's *Histoire des Martyrs*. Finally, in the last chapter, Sancy reveals his doubts about the wisdom of his conversion, but eventually he succumbs to du Perron's reasoning that you must either kill your conscience or let it kill you.

Mention should be made of the manuscript fragment of the *Sancy, Les Avis de Luat*,[3] which seems to form part of the book. In it, Sancy repeats Luat's advice to Sully, that it is extremely wise to know when to pretend to be mad; and he quotes four articles which he subsequently substantiates — the advantages/disadvantages of honesty, wit, courage, and natural ability. Needless to say, it is the innocent who are punished and the wicked rewarded.

III *The Religious Dimension*

Within the pages of the *Sancy* d'Aubigné has crammed much of the dissatisfaction that he had accumulated over the years since Henry IV's accession to the throne. It offers a résumé of many themes which were dear to his heart: the betrayal of the Protestant cause by king and party members alike; the lack of foundation to the Catholic faith; the dangerous arguments used by Catholic theologians, etc. As in many contemporary pamphlets and in keeping with the general tone of d'Aubigné's invective nature, the weaknesses, both moral and doctrinal, of the opposing party are exploited to the full. As commentators of the *Sancy* have shown, there is a close relationship between the allusions in the text and the pamphlet literature or collections composed by Pierre de l'Estoile, allusions which are also to be found scattered through d'Aubigné's other works, especially in this case the books *Misères* and *Princes* in *Les Tragiques,* where the poet has concentrated all his poetic and political venom.

The range of d'Aubigné's points of reference indicates that his satirical eye encompassed more than the conversion of the Sieurs of Sancy and of Sainte Marie du Mont. He raises more fundamental and far-reaching issues lying at the heart of the discord between Catholic and Protestant, such as the role of the pope in the internal affairs of France, always a provocative matter in view of the traditions of the Gallican church. Through Sancy, d'Aubigné mocks the ceremony of submission to the pope undergone by Henry IV by procuration after his acceptance of the Catholic religion. In a manner reminiscent of the Rabelais of the *Quart Livre,* it is suggested that the institution of the pope is dangerous for both religious and political reasons. For the ardent Protestant, the Antichrist that was the pope must have been in league with the devil and d'Aubigné never misses an opportunity of stressing the diabolic influence, going as far as to accuse Alexander VI of having made a Faustian pact with the devil. Although such an accusation can be explained by sixteenth-century attitudes toward the supernatural, we can detect in it an example of d'Aubigné's extreme thought. His tendency to see the contrasting nature of things led him easily to the use of hyperbole. This technique, while serving to vilify the adversary, can make the reader somewhat skeptical of the author's own veracity. In the chapter, *Des Traditions* (*C,* I, 2), for example, d'Aubigné scores a point against Catholicism by allowing Sancy to condemn, albeit indirectly, the church's reliance upon doctrine and scripture as opposed to the Protestants' recognition of Holy Writ alone. The chapter commences well with Sancy's defending the *Index expurgatorius,* purporting to contain a list of passages to be expurgated in the patristic writings; the recanter proceeds to sing the praises of a number of books of doubtful Catholic piety, and then the confession rapidly becomes a scurrilous attack against reputed Catholic saints and a defense of homosexuality. Although the conclusion establishes a subtle link between the past and the present, d'Aubigné, taking the words of the Emperor Julian, shows that, as for the early Christians, the faith of the Huguenots is that of the "gueux et belistres," whereas the Catholic religion, with its financial considerations, is well adapted to the rich, the princes, the nobles, and the financiers. Yet, in spite of the sound theological basis of the thesis, illustrated by the exempla, the attacks on Sponde, Caylus, and the Cardinal de Sourdis destroy the harmony of the naive satirical manner promised in the opening pages.

The fundamental weakness of Catholicism is the appearance of its being a man-made religion. As Montaigne on an allied topic says, "C'est l'homme qui donne et l'homme qui reçoit." Catholic doctrine has evolved by taking into account the frailty of man's will, his leaning toward materialism, and the need to tie his mind down to physical objects rather than let it remain in a field of abstract metaphysics. Thus, Catholic church ceremonies appeal to the senses through the use of incense and iconography; the theologians have rationalized life on earth and have established a system of laws and punishments concerning the spiritual life which have their model in the physical-social fabric. Such procedures, purely arbitrary in d'Aubigné's view, are heavily castigated. The intercession of Saints (*C*, I, 3) is parodied by the suggestion, recalling the concept of "Nature à l'envers" so elaborately developed in *Les Tragiques*, that in the "new" society, the court high dignitaries can be compared with the saints, for the former act as intermediaries: "Ergo il faut que les Saincts et Sainctes fassent leurs affaires du Ciel, comme nous faisons ceux de la Cour" (*C,* 588). Paradise can similarly be considered to be analogous with the court, under the watchful eye of Saint Gabrielle d'Estrées, and this initial conceit is extended greatly by our author, for he seeks to establish the true location of purgatory. This is associated with the *Tiers Parti,* the group of Catholics who supported Henry IV in his claim to the throne and which was formed in 1591 (*C*, I, 4). The image is so labored throughout that its originality, obvious in an earlier chapter, is now overtaxed. The analogy with saints is continued yet further, with the comparison between those who achieve salvation through good works and those who have gained a place for themselves in the French courtly paradise. This theme enables d'Aubigné to air his discontentment by an implied condemnation of the treatment meted out to many faithful servants, such as himself in the king's service, a treatment worthy of "Madame l'Ingratitude." This technique of analogy allows d'Aubigné to satirize economically, if with some loss of dynamism, both the court and Catholic religious practices.

The materialism at which his criticism is leveled is made visible by the handling of the theme of miracles. He gives instances of the uncovering of frauds and charlatanism which were condoned by leading members of the church for their pious utility — "ad pias fraudes." The first examples of madness and self-delusion are well planned, but then the author's love of a tale carries him away and the episode of La Barthelemie (*C*, 602), raised from a false death, is rather out of place in the general context; it would be more suitable for a "recueil de contes." This desire to expand on the structure of an apparently straightforward confession is to be found again in the satirical explanation of Henry III's religious practices where our author embroiders considerably the details of Henry III's homosexual offences. Sexual vilification is also employed to discredit the habit of taking vows, including the extended pun on "oeuvres pies" which revolves around pious works and the piebald effect obtained by the close contact of the black gown of the abbess of Saintes and the white surplice of the bishop as they satisfy their passion.

Materialism is the motivating force too in the chapters devoted to various means of converting men and to the theory of transubstantiation (*C*, I, 9, 10). It is constantly repeated that converts to Catholicism are attracted more by the promise of material gain and reward than by spiritual considerations. With the exploitation of the images of the fishers of men and the process of transubstantiation, d'Aubigné lets his imagination run riot. Transubstantiation is proved, just as the intercession of saints was proved, by analogy between God and the king — why should not God be able to transform when the king has had such great success? We sense another reference to the prevalent state of "nature à l'envers" when, with sparkling irony, d'Aubigné makes Sancy remark:

Today taxes in France have transubstantiated ploughed fields into pasture land, vines into fallow land, workers into beggars, soldiers into thieves, villains into Gentlemen, valets into masters, masters into valets.... Princes' whores are transubstantiated into wives and wives into whores. Pimps go away Princes. (*C*, 621)

Sancy's own rise to fame reflects this same contrast:

I saw myself move from school boy to a counselor; from counselor to an ambassador; from ambassador to a bankrupt; from bankrupt to a thief;

The Satirist

from thief to a financier; from financier to colonel of the Swiss Guards, from colonel to captain and lord of Little Chalon. (*C*, 621-22)

The general criticisms of Catholicism which pervade the first book are accentuated and related more closely to Sancy in the second. There had been several attempts to find an acceptable basis for the unification of the two religions, all, in d'Aubigné's mind, ill-founded and self-interested. His means of ridiculing such attempts is subtly contrived. Through Sancy he highlights a wish by the Catholics to make some superficial concessions in return for the adoption by the Huguenots of more libertine and less austere views:

The other church had to criticize the pomp, the music, the dances, a lot of feasts, the fine large church incomes. The ministers would have been in carriages, followed by many dogs and hunting birds. We would have established free will: and above all we would have expelled this unfortunate discipline which has caused them to lose so many good people. (*C*, 632)

This reproach of lack of gaiety and lack of riches is one frequently delivered by Sancy against the Huguenots. In the examination of his own tergiversations, he reveals his conversions to have beem prompted by opportunism, by the desire to curry the favor of the rising sun of Henry IV (*C*, II, 3); and so, with others at Mantes, he had plotted the overthrow of the Huguenot cause (*C*, II, 4). With an incredible frankness Sancy admits that he has always had "pour but, sans changer, le profit, l'honneur, l'aise et la seurté" (*C*, 641). Although in time of war such advantages might be gained by a Huguenot, in peacetime it was quite different and the contemporary state offered them little:

When I see poor people in their simple fidelity, condemned to be the plaything of the Mighty, farseeing in matters concerning the king divided in their own, taking pity on France when France had none for them, who guard her and receive nothing in return, who fortify her and are chased away from her, I say the *Bezomanos* [farewell] of the Spaniard, taking the view that for the man who has his hands tied for fear of God, and his head bent out of respect for his prince, his peace will never be peace, *sed pactio servitutis,* but a pact of servitude. (*C*, 644)

The Huguenots have that unfortunate failing of placing God's glory above that of the king (*C,* II, 7), and such Huguenot fortitude is well exemplified by d'Aubigné's introduction of his own person into the story, recalling yet again his unheeded words of wisdom to Henry IV.

The structure of Book II is similar to that of the first and Sancy comes back again to the discussion of certain books of contemporary interest (*C,* II, 6) and parodies the so-called martyrs for the Catholic faith (*C,* II, 8) with a long list of farcical deaths including St. Jacques Clément, assassin of Henry III and Monsieur Saint Sponde, "l'yn martyrizé par le Procureur General, l'autre par sa femme" (*C,* 659). In the same way as in Book I, Sancy united the themes of the books in the last chapter; so the final chapter of Book II includes a reflection on the work as a whole. Even Sancy has doubts about what he has done, but du Perron with exemplary, if unchristian, logic, convinces him with the argument that "ceux qui sont morts ont voulu laisser vivre leur conscience, et elle les a tuez. Il la faut donc tuer à bon escient (comme je me vante d'avoir fait), ou l'endormir par stupidité, comme le Baron (de Salignac) ou comme sa femme et les autres par mille petits passetemps d'amour" (*C,* 664).

To be a convert to Catholicism was thus for d'Aubigné to be a traitor to one's cause, to God, to one's country, and to oneself. There is not a line of sympathy for Sancy; he is a fool who is condemned by his own words throughout; he has been foolish and deluded.

Although the structure of the second book resembles that of the first, it does contain a chapter which in some ways does not belong there. The reported conversation between Mathurine the fool and the younger du Perron is in the style of the satirical pamphlet dialogue. Here, as elsewhere in the book, d'Aubigné develops accusations of sexual license, and the exchange between the hermaphroditic du Perron and the lascivious Mathurine about their powers of inciting people to be converted is particularly effective in discrediting the maligned Sainte Marie du Mont and illustrates how d'Aubigné could be both crude and devastating. For the Protestant whose view of vice and virtue was an extreme one, any moral deviation on the Catholic side was immediately seized upon and exploited so as to make the sin seem even greater in the eyes of God and man. Therefore, throughout the *Sancy,* and d'Aubigné's work in general, sexual license is virtually a concomitant of wrong doing.

Here the dialogue which bears little direct relationship with the apparent narrator of the confessions is, in spite of its dynamism and color, in discord with the general presentation. It is as though the dialogue had been written to be published as a separate pamphlet but that then d'Aubigné had changed his mind and had included it in the manuscript of the *Sancy*.

IV *The Success of the* Sancy

Some of the pages of the *Confession* show d'Aubigné at his best. The subtle ironic attack on Catholic institutions and turncoats is worthy of the *Satire Ménippée* and heralds the technique of Voltaire. Not only did the book enjoy several editions in France in the second half of the seventeenth century but it was also translated into English as *Hell Illuminated or Sancy's Roman Catholic Confession, wherein are such Lessons, which if studiously practis'd, 'tis much to be fear'd, the Devil himself will turn Jesuit* (1679). By way of a preface, there is a dialogue between a Roman Catholic and a Protestant, and it is of interest to note that Sancy's wit is mentioned and also the fact that he was in the service of the devil:

Protestant: Indeed I have heard much of this *Sancy,* that he is both a witty, and an impartial Writer ... which makes me wonder, that he being a man of learning, should be drawn aside to be the Devil's Confessour —
Roman Catholic: Oh Sir, 'tis no dishonour to be deluded by the Devil.... Popes and Emperours themselves, have frequently bin gull'd by him, that's more ... but Sancy was not so ... for when he heard his tale, he presently smelt him, and found his Civility to be but an act of Morality, well knowing that had the Devil bin put to have publish'd his Confession in his own name, not one in a Thousand would have believ'd the Father of Lyes —

Had d'Aubigné been more moderate in his handling of the book we would have been provided with a masterly stylistic exercise by which the diabolic reasoning of Sancy and du Perron could have been denounced even more effectively. As it happens, the natural hyperbole of d'Aubigné's pen and temperament very often carries him away from his original purpose and includes material which would have been more at home in other genres. This said, the *Sancy* remains a good example of an effective use of political satire. Had it been published during the author's lifetime, it would no doubt have effectively hurt the converts to Catholicism, incurred their wrath; but one wonders whether d'Aubigné would have found sufficient support among members of his own party to defend his own exaggerated accusations.

The *Sancy* shows an amazing breadth of knowledge of the men, books, events, and ideas involved in the politico-religious power struggle between 1590 and 1604. Written for the most part toward the turn of the century, but revised and altered up until at least 1617, the text provides a wealth of humanist and educated puns, with quotations from Hebrew, Greek, Latin, Italian and Spanish sources. The mixture of the sexual and humanist dimensions in the construction of the chapters is a good reflection of the particular interests of d'Aubigné who was profoundly fascinated by the problems of the body and their intellectual repercussions. Sancy failed because the devil inspired his thoughts and dictated his bodily pleasures.

V Le Divorce Satyrique ou les Amours de la Reyne Marguerite

Published in the seventeenth century, often with the *Confession de Sancy*,[4] the "satirical Divorce" belongs very much to the pamphlet tradition. It is not absolutely certain that it was composed by d'Aubigné, and it was only against their better judgement that Réaume and Caussade decided to publish this "violent and mediocre pamphlet."

Prompted by Henry IV's divorce from Marguerite de Valois to allow him to marry Marie de Medici, the pamphlet is presented as the king's confession about his life with the good Queen Margot. With a naive honesty that can be compared with Sancy's, Henry wishes to defend himself against critics, for some "call him voluptuous, others an atheist, and all ungrateful" (*D,* 656). He dwells upon the similarity between a storm of blood on the Aventine Hill, an omen of the Roman defeat at Canes, and the blood shed during the St. Bartholomew's Day Massacre at the time of his wedding celebrations which was thus an omen of his defeated honor. He proceeds to heap accusation upon accusation against Marguerite, who since the age of twelve had refused nobody in her desire to satisfy her lust. The long list of lovers includes her own brothers, high court officials, and La Molle, whose decapitated head she had borne away in a coach at night and buried with her own hands in the Chapel of St. Martin in Montmartre (*D,* 659) — all this before

The Satirist

her marriage. After her wedding to Henry the same life continued, and Henry asserts that no man of any worth had not been at some time the lover of the queen of Navarre! After her fall from grace in 1583 she was separated from Henry and spent most of her time in the Auvergne, where she slept with her servants and dabbled in black magic, returning to Paris after her divorce with the intention of seeking personal revenge for the murder of her valet-lover St. Julien. In spite of Henry's apology for the length of his exposé we sense that this pamphlet is particularly bent on the moral destruction of the former queen of Navarre. Her life becomes a symbol of sin and sexual license. This work has played a great role in influencing the opinion of posterity against Marguerite. At times, there is a certain coarseness in the description as when, to stress her sacrilege on taking communion, she is described as: "... impudently daring for several years to take communion three times a week in a mouth as made-up as is her heart, her face plastered and covered with rouge, with a large uncovered bosom which would be better and more appropriately compared with a backside than with breasts" (*D*, 676).

Like Faeneste Marguerite is presented as being only concerned with outward appearances: "In fact all that she does is but show and ostentation, without any spark of devotion or piety" (*D*, 682). The overall picture is far too black and pessimistic; if d'Aubigné is indeed the author of the pamphlet, then his characteristic defect of extreme exaggeration is certainly inherent in this work. And yet it is essential to place any pamphlet in its historical context, to realize that now we can read through these literary productions without any of the sectarian fury of the past. D'Aubigné lived in violent times and used his pen as violently, so as to convey his point of view as strongly as he felt it.

VI Le Caducée ou l'Ange de Paix

The caduceus, associated with Mercury, was the title given by d'Aubigné to the political pamphlet he produced about the Assembly of the Reformed church held at Saumur from May 27 to September 12, 1611.[5] The Assembly was ostensibly to elect new general deputies who, since the Edict of Nantes in 1598, were supposed to be the negotiators between the crown and the Reformed churches. D'Aubigné took an active part in the Assembly which sought a return to the original draft terms of the Edict of Nantes and new assurances of safety for the Reformed churches now that Henry IV was dead. The demands of the Huguenots met resistance from the queen mother, Marie de Medici, and she was eventually obliged to deliver an ultimatum to the Assembly that they either agree or disband. The deadlock was finally broken by Du Plessis-Mornay who persuaded the Assembly to elect the deputies. Some of the Huguenots, following the duke of Bouillon's example, had acquiesced in the queen's wishes to avoid a split in the churches; others in the minority, including the duke of Rohan and d'Aubigné, had agreed on a policy of firm opposition. D'Aubigné considered the first group to constitute the party of the *Prudents* and the second that of the *Fermes,* and the synods at Thouars and at Privas in 1612 only increased his mistrust of the former. Du Plessis-Mornay had to try to heal the wounds of division in the party, and it was against such a reconciliatory background that d'Aubigné's document is to be placed, for it argues more in favor of the *Fermes*.

VII *Content*

The pamphlet takes the form of an enquiry, of a *procès-verbal,* held by a minister of the Reformed church who wishes to examine the points of view of the two opposing Huguenot parties, so as to satisfy his own troubled conscience. He has listened to their laments and told them of the wrath of God to be seen in the current division. The minister narrates how he first visits a nobleman of great authority and experience and who had been present throughout the Assembly at Saumur. The defense of his "Prudent" policy is well constructed: he argues that had he wanted personal gain, he would have opted for the hard Huguenot line of a state within a state; he desires peace and is against the personal ambition of Huguenot leaders. If the queen chose to reward them with presents for their loyalty, it was in no way indicative of their having been traitors but merely a sign of the queen's munificence. The narrator proposes the name of *Prudents* rather than the condemning epithets of treacherous, mercenary, perfidious, and corrupt; and on the other hand, *Fermes* in the place of incendiaries, zealots, warmongers, troublemakers, and rebels.

Two days later, the pastor visits a nobleman from the Saintonge, connected for the past twenty years with the Protestant Assemblies.

He is above reproach and had nothing to gain from war unless it be the disturbance of his peace, worldly comforts, and pastimes. He is opposed to war, especially to civil war, and claims that the accusation of warmongering comes from those who associate the court sympathizers of the party with peace and the provincial Huguenots with war. There follows an examination of the three theses which are the points of difference between the two parties. The first thesis states (a) "that the Huguenots can preserve their lives and their possessions by inspiring pity in others" and (b) "that they will be preserved through mutual fear [*mutua formidine*]." It is argued that (a) is difficult to ascertain and that in the case of (b) experience has shown that mutual fear is a war deterrent and an agent in favor of peace.

The second thesis proposes (a) "that the Huguenots' adversaries no longer wish to extirpate them" and (b) "that they do." The former proposition (a) is not true if consideration is given to the assasination of Henry IV, for he was said to have been killed because he protected the Protestants. The third thesis asserts (a) "that the Huguenot order cannot be right and stay within the state" and (b) "that it can be right and can remain within the state." The answer to this difference had already been provided in several books, such as the *Vindiciae contra Tyrannos*, attributed to Du Plessis-Mornay, and what more proof was needed than the fact that so many princes had supported the party in its fight against tyranny? It was injustice which had forced them to take up arms and thus to form the party:

You will find that the unjust burnings and massacres have provoked men to arm; the armed men formed the party, the treacheries of St. Bartholomew's Day have brought about places being held to ransom, those divisions that were fomented in the provinces created a protector, the division at Saumur changed of necessity the curtailment of the synods into councils of war. (*CA*, 86)

The Saintangeois finishes on a note of refusal to accept the line followed by the *Prudents:* the pastor stresses the need for Christian charity and peace. The gentleman's cousin arrives for dinner and it is soon evident that he supports the *Prudents*. The two cousins argue over the legality of the arrest of the ladies of the Rohan family who had since been released. The Huguenot minister then reports the after-dinner conversation verbatim, the interlocutors being *Le Prudent, Le Ferme,* and himself, *Le Modeste.* As the discussion proceeds, *Le Modeste* takes the role of arbiter in the exchanges of accusation: *Le Prudent* claims to represent obedience and *Le Ferme,* disobedience. *Le Ferme* accuses *Le Prudent* of sacrificing his principles by agreeing to acknowledge the church to be only "Prétendue Refformee" (*CA,* 94), and maintains that you cannot always rely upon the king's word. *Le Prudent* admits that some of his party received gifts from royalty for services rendered but also some of the *Fermes* received state pensions. The exchanges become more and more heated, yet reveal sound logic. *Le Ferme* goes as far as to liken the *Prudents* to the Jesuits (*CA,* 104), and finally calls for a general assembly to settle their differences (*CA,* 106). The *Modeste* concludes that the national synod must decide in favor of one view or the other.

The pastor returns home and en route meets the duke of Rohan who reaffirms his desire for the good of the party, and states how God's honor is more important than earthly honors. The pastor gives thanks to God when he hears that at the Synod of Privas in August, 1612, agreement had been reached between the two parties, and the pamphlet finishes with a statement of the purity of God's church.

VIII Originality of Presentation

The interest of the work for the modern reader is an historical one, in that it throws light upon a difficult period of Huguenot history. The tone of the work contrasts greatly with that of *Le Divorce Satirique* and *La Confession de Sancy.* D'Aubigné produces a pamphlet which appears to come from the pen of an impartial man, in so far as he can remain impartial. Stylistically, *Le Caducée* is to be contrasted with the *Sancy,* in the same way that the *Histoire universelle* can be compared with *Les Tragiques.* Critics have suggested that *Le Prudent* represents Du Plessis-Mornay, and *Le Ferme* and *Le Modeste* aspects of d'Aubigné himself. There can be no doubt that the presentation of the "Gentilhomme du Xaintonge" with the reference to his "exelans jardinages' and "une maisonnette de plaisir qui est au bout de son parterre' (*CA,* 78), is reminiscent of the simply country life led by such a man as Enay in *Les Avantures du Baron de Faeneste.* The theories, which will occur later in d'Aubigné's political writings, are expounded with clarity and force. Although we feel that d'Aubigné would have preferred the view of the *Fermes* to prevail, it is interesting to note how the final outcome of the pamphlet is the reiteration of the belief in the need for a united party so as, no doubt, to be better equipped to withstand the adversary in the future.

The whole text is placed under the sign of peace and unity, the title, with its mixture of classical and Christian connotations heralds the irenic moves of the *Modeste.* The book opens with a quotation from the Beatitudes, "Blessed are the peacemakers...," and terminates with the closing lines of the Lord's Prayer. In his interventions, *Le Modeste* invokes the true Christian spirit of charity and peace and provides the link between the episodes.

The use of reported speech and dialogue to discriminate differing points of view was well established by the end of the sixteenth century. There are obvious advantages to be gained from a Socratic type of discussion, and we find such authors as Tahureau, Henri Estienne, and works such as *La Satire Ménippée* and countless pamphlets of the turn of the century which exploit the technique. D'Aubigné has succeeded in distinguishing between his characters and in capturing the unctuous tone of the *Prudent,* who seeks to explain away his apparently cowardly actions and attitudes, thus establishing a good linguistic contrast with the fiery and impassioned words of *Le Ferme.*

The dialogue is handled skilfully and d'Aubigné has introduced some variety into the responses. They are not all of the same length, which can be a boring characteristic of some of the more philosophical contemporary dialogues. There is a certain dynamism and freshness which brings to life the dramatic exchanges of viewpoint — as, for example, in the following lines which have a stichomythian form:

The Prudent. Those are your suspicions. Who could find it odd that the queen followed the advice of those who were in the midst of the matter?
The Firm: Let us say they were working for her.
The Prudent: And for whom else? Are we not bound to work for our king?
The Firm: It is to serve him, to grant justice to the plaintiffs.
The Prudent: It is to serve him better to prevent the pleas.
The Firm: Yes, by preventing the reasons for the pleas. (*CA,* 105)

The irony and the humor, often of a scabrous nature, which are ever-present and account for much of the charm of the *Sancy* and of the *Divorce Satyrique,* are absent from *Le Caducée.* Here we are face to face with a grave problem treated in a grave, yet lively manner. D'Aubigné in such a work reveals his genius as a man of clear thought and forceful literary expression. One can only conjecture the political and literary influence the pamphlet might have had, had it been published before the nineteenth century.

CHAPTER 6

The King and the People

YEARS of civil strife left their mark on d'Aubigné, and it is not surprising that he explored the relationship between the king and his people. Although there is some doubt about the actual date of the composition of d'Aubigné's two tracts concerning this relationship,[1] it is highly probable that they are to be read together. As Armand Garnier remarks "*The Treaty on the mutual right of Kings and their subjects* lays down the law, the *Treaty on the Civil Wars* applies it to particular circumstances, to a given case. This is all the difference there is between the two works. The second provides us with an example, and illustration of the political doctrine exposed in the first...."[2] If we accept that they were written shortly after d'Aubigné's arrival in exile in Geneva (1620–1622), their composition would coincide with the occupation of the Valtellina by Spanish troops and the reintroduction of Catholicism into Béarn, both of which events confirmed d'Aubigné's fear of a Catholic threat to the existence of Protestantism, as is amply witnessed by his correspondence of the period.

I   Du Debvoir mutuel des Roys et des Subjects

The treatise is in the form of an answer to certain theses d'Aubigné had received and which had been circulated in Guyenne. He reveals himself to be a worthy successor to the Protestant apologists of a previous age, when the scars of the memories of the St. Bartholomew Day massacre had not healed. Mention is made of several important theoretical studies: François Hotman's *Franco-Gallia* (1573), Du Plessis-Mornay's *Vindiciae contra tyrannos* (1579), as well as Etienne de la Boétie's youthful essay, *Discours sur la servitude volontaire,* which had already been exploited by the Protestants in *Le Resveille-Matin* of 1574. The theses discussed are of a general but topical nature: (1) If the treaties, contracts and agreements between the prince and subjects are binding on the prince; (2) By what legitimate means a prince can be forced to observe the agreements and promises made with his subjects; (3) What guarantees and assurances the people can ask of its prince for the observation of the agreements and the promises; (4) If the prince can, without prejudice to his authority, treat with his subjects about the means necessary to realize completely what has been granted and agreed by both sides, and to agree about the nature of the guarantees promised by the prince; (5) If the subjects, having the prince's permission, can be certain of being able to (or can continue to hold the assembly called by the prince) advise on the legitimate means of righting the infringement to the promises of their prince and of renewing the guarantees and assurances that the prince has given them. The answers to these logical and legal questions examined by the author are addressed to three types of person: the party's adversaries and those outside the party, those who somewhat simplemindedly seek information, and the hypocrites who pretend to do so (Chapter I).

In his reply to the adversaries of the Protestant church, d'Aubigné is content to quote the example of the Sorbonne which, during the troubles of the League resisted the king and supported the people of Paris who took the law into their own hands, even going so far as to impose a temporary canonization on the regicide Jacques Clément (Chapter II).

The reasons d'Aubigné provides for the unintelligent who require explanation are given on three levels, the theological, the jurisprudential, and the constitutional. With a great show of his mastery of biblical exegesis, the author marshals his arguments well. Alleged biblical support for absolute kingship is based, he claims, on a misinterpretation of Holy Scripture. As proof of God's control of kings and as justification of Protestant resistance, David and his adventures with Saul are quoted. The horrors of the St. Bartholomew Day Massacre are recalled, as, for example, when Charles IX took random shots at the so-called heretics. D'Aubigné sees a straight parallel to be drawn between the Huguenots and David: "Like David we have taken flight to foreign kingdoms and even over the seas; like him we have hidden away our lives in caves and forests and there presented our hearts and our requests to God for His sake and then for our own" (Chapter III). Furthermore, the Protestants only took up arms after suffering tremendous atroci-

The King and the People

ties. Despite this justification of the Protestant cause the author repeats his belief that the monarchy is the most honorable and excellent form of rule, when it is supported by protective measures which will prevent its becoming a tyranny.

The omnipotent prince cannot base his power on ancient laws (Chapter IV). In fact they stress that the prince's authority comes from the people. Constitutionally only the just king can be supported and not the tyrant (Chapter V). A tyrant can be defined not simply as a violent and extreme ruler but one who abuses royal power. The members of the Reform were forced to offer resistance by injustice and "then gradually the sufferers became defenders, persecution became war and lambs were transformed into lions...." It is indeed a felony for the king to try and exert an influence over the people's religious conscience which depends upon God alone. He concludes by quoting the words of the doge of Venice to Henry III, that it should not be necessary for a king to have to give his word, that he should be able to rule by law but, if he gives his word, then he should not violate it.

The hypocrites who compare obedience to the king with obedience to God, thereby exalt the state and degrade religion. They are given short shrift by the angry Huguenot, and he suggests that they are twisting their conscience for their own advantage (Chapter VI).

The final chapter gives the corollary of d'Aubigné's statements — the king who breaks his contract with the people also breaks theirs with him. It is incumbent upon the prince to respect his guarantees, and if he does not, then the people must not support him. The author, turning his attention to the contemporary state of France, deduces that the Protestants are surrounded by enemies under the reign of injustice. The consolation for the faithful is to be found in the next world, which is the fount of joy and perfection: "The port of all our storms is therefore in the haven and lap of death, which, if it is completely scorned by us, can no longer frighten us by its means" (Chapter VII).

The style of the work is that of a reasoned legal document. Drawing upon his own culture and borrowing from other Protestant and Catholic apologists, d'Aubigné creates an ardent defense of Protestant politics. As is often the case, the author has little patience with the opponents of the true church or with those who have betrayed their conscience. He seeks to establish an ancestry for the Huguenot resistance in the Old Testament, and thus recalls the main themes of *Les Tragiques*. On several occasions he turns to his own *Histoire universelle* for an explanation of a point or to elaborate his thought. It is implicit that his conception of the state is one which is in accordance with divine teaching: kings are at the mercy of God and responsible to, and for, their people. Religious conscience is a matter to be settled between man and God, and it is not for the king to impose his will on his subjects. This gives force to d'Aubigné's contention that the pressure employed to reinstate Catholic practices among the Huguenots constitutes an unjust act.

II Traité sur les Guerres Civiles

Written with the firm conviction that there was a gigantic Catholic plot to stifle the Protestant movement, this treatise examines the contemporary state of affairs and makes gloomy forecasts. D'Aubigné was even encouraged to keep his document secret until further proof of what he foresaw was available. He has little respect for advisers who take the king at his word, and claims that there are four bodies who oppose extreme action: the parliament, the large towns, the elders of the privy council, and those who curry favor. Against arguments from these four bodies supporting peace, d'Aubigné has always opposed the tyrannical power that the king's confessors wield over him and the fact that the nobles are more content to be subservient to favor than to be rivals. It was while such discussions had been protracted that the devil had got to work and extended his vile influence. He would have destroyed the faithful already if God had not sought to maintain truth (Chapter I).

Royal persecution of the Huguenots had been helped by the shortsighted members of the party. Already in 1611 at Saumur, the queen mother had started the process of undermining Protestant strength, and since then the situation had only worsened, with the Huguenot strongholds falling one after another under Catholic control (Chapter II). The "faux pasteurs" failed to heed the warnings of critics such as d'Aubigné, who told them of the dangers of betraying their conscience:

Those very people have formed a hatred for those minds which, on seeing this decadence, chastised them for their curly hair, their starched clothing, their ridiculous conversations, the loose garters and exorbitant clothes both of themselves and their wives. They dubbed these critics, who vividly pointed out the state in which we find ourselves at the moment, bitter and violent; they even went as far as to call the "fermes" turbulent and muddlers.... (Chapter II)

There may reign an impression of peace and tolerance but it is false, for underneath there is a desire to encourage the Huguenots to commit crimes against their conscience (Chapter III). Their adversaries claim that the Protestants have lost their old zeal, but God, d'Aubigné suggests, has shown that this is not true, for not only do the barbaric persecutions continue, but there are still examples of firm constancy in the faith. It is the atheists, like the persecutors of the early church, who try and prove that resistance to the tyrant is wrong, even if it is for God's sake. They are mistaken, for God has not abandoned his own:

In this little treatise and in the treatment which begins with France, you will see that God's spirit has always had its strength, that He communicates this to His church and then He honors it with past triumphs: He is not weary of her, He holds her by the hand and will raise her up over her enemies. (Chapter III)

As a major proof of the Catholic plot, there features the anecdote concerning Gaspar Baronius, nephew of the cardinal, who turned against Catholicism after being called upon to be one of the seven judges of the "petit capucin" in Rome (Chapter IV). He defected, contacted Lesdiguières and thence went to Paris where at the duke of Bouillon's residence, in the presence of d'Aubigné and Feuguère, he revealed his papers.[3] They contained two dossiers, one entitled *Artis pacis apud Rhaetos,* the other, *Artes belli.* Therein were details of the events which had since occurred in the Poitou and caused bloodshed in Europe, thus giving adequate proof of the generally premeditated nature of what had happened. They form part of what the author terms the "grand design" which was to bring Europe under the domination of a single bishop and of a single king, entailing the suppression of all heresy in favor of the Catholic church, and all republics in favor of the princes. Switzerland was not to be spared, and the property of the Protestant princes was to be used to provide money to fight the Huguenots. The Jesuits and the Franciscans were in the plot, and, as an example of Louis XIII's support for the "design," he quotes from a letter the king addressed to the pope, pleading for the Jesuits and the canonization of Ignatius Loyola.

Thoroughly convinced of the truth of the "grand design" (Chapter V) the author warns England of the danger of the Jesuits and laments the fact that Holland, Switzerland, and France are not aware of their precarious position.

The age of the Antichrist has arrived (Chapter VI), and by ruse a hundred Huguenot strongholds have been lost. It is the duty of the Protestants to resist and in God's name d'Aubigné appeals to them: "Here Heaven is speaking to you, Christian knights, heaven is arousing you with its thunder; do not fear that it will make you guilty if you shoulder arms to go to the help of the lambs of God" (Chapter VI).

It is their duty to defend the oppressed and combat the injustice of the tyrant. God commands both spiritual and temporal arms and, with the memory of the 1572 massacre, they should call to mind the fact that: "All things will abound when your sins no longer hide the face of Him who has the victories in His hand."

Although it is difficult to substantiate the proofs proposed by d'Aubigné,[4] it is obvious that he was totally committed to an action of resistance in the belief that the true religion was in danger. Embittered by his own experiences, he was never to abdicate his position as the inexorable defender of Protestant rights. In these two treatises, we see the elaboration of a faith and of a political point of view which he had possessed from the signing of the Edict of Nantes onward. He was never to abandon his hatred of the Jesuits, his mistrust of Catholic kings, or his suspicion of the Papacy. There exists between the *Debvoir mutuel* and the *Traité sur les Guerres civiles* a relationship which is similar to that found between the *Histoire universelle* and *Les Tragiques*. In the former d'Aubigné strives to be impartial and, although in the *Traité* he does provide what he considers to be undeniable proof, it is an emotional, indeed impassioned appeal that he makes to the Protestants.

At times, his rhetoric resembles that of the fiery Huguenot preacher who contrasts the kingdom of God in heaven with the kingdom of man on earth. There is running through it this deep-rooted conviction that God will not desert the Huguenot cause; that, as always, truth will out and eventually win the day. One can but admire, if not support, the single-mindedness and the enthusiasm of a man who dedicated his whole life to the defense of his religion and truth. He possessed something of the fire of the social reformers of the eighteenth century. Had his interests lain more in social matters than in religious ones, then there is no doubt that his name and his work would be better remembered today.

CHAPTER 7

"The Meditations on the Psalms"

NEITHER the Catholic nor the Protestant poets could claim the monopoly of devotional poetry in France.[1] In the second half of the sixteenth century it underwent a sort of revival which coincided with the Wars of Religion, no doubt "due in part to the universal need for 'consolation' at a time of universal affliction."[2] A number of leading Protestant men of letters turned their attention to the psalms and wrote long meditations on them. It was above all the penitential psalms which they studied and in which they sought consolation for the vicissitudes of their earthly life. The major Huguenot authors in this domain were Théodore de Bèze, Jean de Sponde, Du Plessis-Mornay, and Agrippa d'Aubigné. Although there exist a number of similarities between d'Aubigné's work and that of his contemporaries, his production possesses its own individuality and his meditations are characterized by his close adhesion to the text and by his desire to expound it in a didactic manner.[3]

The six meditations composed between 1588 and 1626 appeared in the *Petites oeuvres meslées,* published by Pierre Aubert in Geneva in 1630. They may even have been published the year before but, if that is the case, then that edition has completely disappeared.[4] In his preface, the author states the diverse reasons which have prompted him to compose his meditations: the materialism of his contemporaries on the one hand, and on the other, those vain minds which proclaim that God's word is in an unpolished style and can have a pernicious effect. His aim, therefore, is to show the beauties of Holy Scripture, to bring comfort to those who love God, and to get his readers to detach their minds from earthly things and to raise them up to God who is the fount of all mercy. The author emphasizes that he has left aside the issues of religious controversy, a statement which is hardly borne out on reading the meditations, as they contain a number of references to the injustices committed against the Huguenots which are denounced throughout his work. Nevertheless, there is one matter on which he begs to differ, and this concerns the pronoun used when addressing God. Following Ronsard and the Pléiade in their style of royal address, d'Aubigné decides to use the "tu" form for God rather than "vous" since God "est un et seul."

The meditations have both a particular and a general application. Each one is preceded by a short introductory paragraph giving the "Occasion et Argument," then follows the psalm or verset of the psalm taken from the Geneva Bible of 1588, which forms the basis of the meditation, and then there is the meditation proper.

I Meditation I

The first meditation, on Psalm 133, was composed at the request of Henry IV who wanted d'Aubigné to produce something uncynical on the sweet pleasures of peace, for the christening of the future Louis XIII in 1606. The commentary is essentially on the role of peace, "le souverain bien de la vie humaine," but the author develops, with the help of the biblical text, the image of the body politic, for peace: "It is like the precious ointment upon the head, that ran down the beards, even Aaron's beard: that went down to the skirts of his garments." The head represents the king, the tiara represents the type of king; he is the eyes and the power of the state; his beard and his neck symbolize the ecclesiastics; the arms and the sword belt, the nobility; the legs and feet, the people. All participate in the running of the state, the ecclesiastics by their advice, acting as intermediaries between heaven and earth, the nobleman with his blood, and the populace with its brawn. This emphasis on the close relationship between ruler and ruled is reminiscent of the author's more formal treatises on the monarchical system or his satirical outbursts against evil rulers in *Misères* and *Princes*. He maintains, for example, that the "precious ointment" or myrrh is destined to prevent corruption in the hands of a good king as distinct from the tyrant: "By this means just as tyrants make living bodies into rotting carcasses of state, the kings who are the fathers of them, convert a state which they find in pieces and rotting into a body full of life and a triumphant kingdom" (*M,* 500). This concretization of abstract concepts into a practical application is a feature of the art of the preacher. It is continued when d'Aubigné takes up the second image, that of the fertile hills of Sion and Hermon contrasted with the sterile flanks of Basan. The mountains epitomize the state and in France, "ce Royaume affligé," he has seen heaven vent its wrath against the iniquity of the country by sending calamity upon calamity: "It is because of this that we have seen the palaces changed into hovels, the galleries of Fontainebleau into stables, the gardens into pasture land, the fountains into a mire for pigs, and the hall of the Louvre into gallows (*M,* 502). Now all is changing because not only have the princes made peace among themselves but heaven has made its peace with the princes. The effective role of the great king is compared with that of the sun who draws his strength from the people and redistributes it about him. The meditation at this point ceases to be concerned with earthly things and turns to our spiritual relationship to God. For although he has spoken of the blessings of heaven, d'Aubigné now feels that it is time to mention the punishments which await those whose hearts have rebelled against God: here, as in his correspondence, d'Aubigné quotes from *Les Tragiques,* illustrating yet again how that work contains the quintessence of his religious thought. The only true peace is to be found through the church; and the meditation ends on an appeal for gratitude for the hand that has brought peace, for a continued strength in the faith and in the general love of mankind. There is present the suggestion that the Protestants must take care not to lose sight of their cause and allow themselves to be lulled into the ways of Cain, for they will be responsible for their actions on the Day of Judgment.

II *Meditation II*

Addressed to an important Protestant nobleman, the meditation on Psalm 84 is aimed at consoling him in the light of his complaint that great nations and people are ungrateful toward their servants and that virtuous conduct only serves to provoke the wrath and hatred of others. As is his wont, d'Aubigné follows closely the text of the psalm, expanding upon it and incorporating in his commentary a number of phrases lifted directly from the Old Testament, which serve to provide a truly religious cadre for his exposition. The reader is confronted by the primordial contrast to be found so often in d'Aubigné's religious works, that of heaven and

"The Meditations on the Psalms"

earth. There is only one true justice and that is God's — God's greatness is immortal and cannot be compared with the mortal splendor of man's efforts. In the midst of persecution the faithful can take refuge in their own hearts which are the private living place of the Holy Spirit in them. In violent terms he condemns those who have forsaken and have been forsaken by God:

These weak hearts which God allowed to melt by abandoning them, because he was abandoned by them; these breasts which are neither holy nor temples, but cess pools of foul water and cowardice, have changed the violence, with which their fathers captured the kingdom of heaven, into halfhearted conduct which God vomits from His mouth, into mortal coldness, into the darkness of the Egyptians: darkness I say, which is caused by the absence of the fire which before was the sign of the presence of God. (*M*, 511)

He seeks a precedent for the conduct of the Huguenots in the midst of their affliction in the practices of the Jews on their way into exile in Babylon, and he sees the abandonment of faith and law by his contemporaries as a reflection of Israel's own behavior. He calls for a moral revival to reinstate the church of God on earth. Those who have suffered from false accusations and ingratitude should take solace in the fact that God will reward them: "Heaven, which is never ungrateful, repairs the errors of the earth, and when earthly sources are lacking, opens up its own to reward the suffering of him who places his hope in the right place" (*M*, 514). The theme of "être" and "paraître" reappears for, after asking God to deliver us from the assaults of the devil, he states that our desires tend toward two goals, one being glory and the other, safety. These are contrary in effect, for "le paroistre appelle à soi la veuë et l'envie, et la seurté fuit tous les deux." The princes are incapable of protecting those they have elevated, for they are likely to suffer the fate of Achitophel or Hamon. God alone protects man, and he works in devious ways. He has protected Elizabeth of England after her humiliation, and God's own son was subjected to scorn and ill-treatment before he triumphed in glory. God alone is perfect, and even those religious leaders of the past are not without their blemishes. The meditation ends with a reaffirmation of trust in God and of a belief in the rewards of God's grace. In his final paragraph the author adds a personal note indicating that the meditation is a statement of his own creed as well as being a letter of consolation for the dedicatee.

III *Meditation III*

The occasion of this meditation of Psalm 73 is similar to that of the previous one. The author's ostensible aim was to bring comfort to certain Gascon noblemen, among others Viscount Gourdon, who, after great services rendered to Henry IV, found themselves impoverished, unrewarded for their pains. This is yet again a theme dear to d'Aubigné's own heart, for it was one of his grievances against the king. The author stresses the need for strong faith in God when the wicked are seen to be rewarded and the good punished. It is a human tendency to envy the good fortune of the wicked but one should remember the Lord's Prayer — "Thy will be done.... Thy Kingdom come" — thus death becomes desirable to the afflicted, and one should not forget that the higher the wicked rise, the greater will be their fall, for eternal death awaits them. Adopting the tone of the lamentations of the prophets of the Old Testament, d'Aubigné personifies the church and makes her review the situation, making ample reference to Holy Scripture. From the miseries of the terrestrial condition he looks in ecstasy toward heaven and God:

It is the greatness, the splendor and the duration of His eternal graces which must make all physical and mental suffering a pleasure and pleasant the threshold of death: all sadnesses become joys, debasement, and elevation when compared one with another; the shadow of the grave is the entrance into unspeakable light, the earth is but a speck to him who grasps the immensity of the firmament: and so there is nothing in the world which could rightly be called misfortune, which should be feared, complained of, and abhorred by him who can be aware of the joys to come, except that which could deprive us of them or place them farther away from our reach. (*M,* 531)

God is invoked to strengthen his arm in the good fight for his church, and once again a text from *Jugement* is quoted to illustrate his argument. The meditation ends on a note of complete abandon to the mercy of God; afflictions are seen as a means of gaining life in Christ through earthly death, for then the true believer will discover real joys and things "... that eye has not seen, that ear has

"The Meditations on the Psalms" 133

not heard, that no mind has been great enough to understand nor anyone able to desire" (*M,* 535).

IV Meditation IV

Psalm 51, which forms the basis of this text, was one of the penitential psalms commented upon, among others, by Théodore de Bèze and Du Plessis-Mornay. This meditation was composed probably in 1588 for Henry IV who was in a penitent frame of mind at the Assembly of La Rochelle in November of that year in the face of accusations of pandering to the Catholics and of allowing his private life to be so expensive. Following closely the text of the original psalm, d'Aubigné's commentary is also in the first person, and by a similarity of style and tone both psalm and commentary are inextricably linked. The author has recaptured the spirit of the original and has, thanks to his biblical scholarship, expanded it into a full self-commination. It moves from a general confession of his sins, admitting the influence of the devil and seeing himself as the lowest of men — "moi qui suis un ver, et non point un homme, opprobre des hommes et le mespris du peuple" — toward a recognition of God's goodness. He has raised him up to kingship and to a position of being a "pescheur prescheur et pescheur d'hommes." The sinner calls upon God's help to give him strength, to remove his confidence from earthly honors, to renew his faith and build up the church. God's kindness is to be seen in the way he has chosen France as the elected kingdom for his people and shown them the true religion. The final note is one of entire dedication of his life to God, ready to be sacrificed for the sake of truth and His name.

V Meditation V

Composed five years after the death of his wife, Suzanne de Lezay, in 1595, the meditation on Psalm 88 is extremely personal and poignant. It presents a picture of utter and complete misery. The author gives vent to feelings which, although they reflect those of the psalmist, are piercingly sincere. The ancients invented the Furies to suggest that man was worried by the memory of the important affairs of the day, and the Christian d'Aubigné too is submerged by his memories and he bathes his couch in tears. His mind and grief give him no rest, and he confesses that he is and has been a sinner. His other afflictions, exile and personal suffering, can be compared in no way with this separation from his other half. In a lyrical turn of phrase the bereft husband expresses the sanctity of this marriage: "Nous allions unis à ta maison, et de la nostre, voire de la chambre et du lict faisions un temple à ton honneur." Like the other meditations, however, this one closes with the author placing his whole trust in God. He uses words which recall the last lines of *Les Tragiques* as he exclaims:

I have no more powerful words, nor violent enough ones to express my misfortunes. Oh Lord, you know, since they are by your hand. In the midst of my anguish I remain in ecstasy, on my knees, my sighs filling the air, my eyes turned to Heaven, my heart for you; raise it up, my Lord, in the hope of salvation through you. (*M,* 556)

VI *Meditation VI*

It was to Psalm 16 that d'Aubigné turned toward the end of his life when, in 1626, he wished to write a meditation for the benefit of the family of an Italian refugee in Geneva, Horace Micheli, who was at death's door.[5] In times of danger men whose hearts are in the world turn to other men, the children of God turn to Him and trust in His great mercy. This comparison between the ways of material men and God's children is extended, stressing the great differences which exist between them. D'Aubigné shows his partisanship for the Huguenot cause by emphasizing the value of the teachings of St. Paul and in denouncing idolatry, the latter so often associated in d'Aubigné's mind with Catholicism. Little importance is attached to the persecutions and the material discomfort suffered in God's name, for "man doth not live by bread alone, but by every word that proceedeth out of the mouth of the Lord doth man live" (Deut. 8.3). God is to be thanked for his gifts; the wicked may gnash their teeth in the midst of their prosperity, but the persecuted faithful are joyous to suffer for God's sake. He knows what is best and how to convert evil into good:

He has a store of infirmities, wounds, hatreds, quarrels, illnesses, poverty, anguish, prisons, torture, and mutilation of limbs to use against us, through which He inclines us toward complete steadfastness, cure, friendships, agreements, health, abundance, joy, freedom, pleasure, and complete perfection: and these things are turned to good when by this strange means the body is tamed to follow its soul freely; everything is in harmony; the soul is rich in piety, the mind in judgment, the heart in love, and the hand ready to commit a charitable act.... (*M*, 567)

The Christian believes that the tomb is not the end, and looks forward to the resurrection of the dead. Although the body may decay there remains the immortal seed which can reconstitute the whole. Through disintegration is achieved a renovation — an argument the author outlines in the last book of *Les Tragiques*. God will show us the straight and narrow path which leads to eternal salvation.

In an interesting parallel with ancient mythology, the author sees a close relationship between the Christian life and the trials and tribulations of Aeneas before reaching Latium: "nous tendons au Latium, où les destinées nous monstrent une demeure tranquille et asseurée." The tone resembles even more that of a sermon, when d'Aubigné denounces human desires as deceptive, whereas only heavenly ones are infallible and can become real pleasures. In a passionate oratorical finale the author sings the praises of that heavenly life which is so desirable. He ends on an ecstatic note, repeating the same phrases as in the penultimate paragraph of the third meditation.

VII *Aspects of the Style*

A number of close links between *Les Tragiques* and the *Méditations* have already been indicated. There exists not only a spiritual connection but also one of outlook and poetic imagery. D'Aubigné flaunts his broad knowledge of the Old Testament and that conception of history which saw in contemporary events a reflection of those to be found in the early days of the biblical past. There are constant references to Old Testament leaders, provided as examples to the Huguenots. The author's familiarity with the style of the psalmists allows him to use the words of the Bible with his own so that it is not always easy to distinguish one from the other.[6] As in *Les Tragiques* he seems to be inspired by an all-pervading religious spirit, if not of prophesy, at least of deep-rooted conviction and sincerity. His avowed aim in the preface is to show the beauties of the language of Holy Scripture; he borrows frequently from the 1588 Geneva Bible, the psalms in the versions of Théodore de Bèze and Clément Marot, and supplements them with his own renderings of the original texts. There is a movement toward the concretization of abstract concepts; the poetic images of the original psalm are sometimes explained in political terms as in Meditation I, or in Meditation III where the chain in "pride compasseth them about as a chain," is interpreted as a military decoration awarded for the persecution of the faithful. In Meditation III also the church is personified and given voice, a technique fully developed in *Les Tragiques*. As in that work, the basic opposition running through "The Meditations" is the one between heaven and earth. It is an antithesis which is visible both on the ideological level and in the imagery. Satan is frequently mentioned as having been at work on earthly man; he provokes corruption and evil and this is opposed to the everlasting beauties of God's kingdom. As is common in d'Aubigné's other works and in those of his contemporaries, there is a certain exaggeration in the descriptions with a penchant for the macabre. God's temple in the hearts of the faithful has been replaced by another: "These first temples have been knocked down by death and in their shameful place we can see only hovels, the lairs of serpents, gremlins, vices, and infections. These pigs, into whom the devils threw themselves, are bodies without soul or life" (*M*, 511). Elsewhere the penitent laments his sins: "I could only bring sin upon sin, for the best actions of man are foul and stinking like the menses of women" (*M*, 539). And later, on a similar theme, he remarks: "You have taken Lazarus already stinking from the grave: I confess that I am completely foul and that the stench of my sins is unbearable for me" (*M*, 552).

Throughout there is a sense of logical development, often prompted by the structure of the psalm, and also by the leanings of the author toward a sermon-type of meditation. He muses on the teachings of Holy Scripture and wishes to convert and instruct his readers. He gives the impression of being divinely inspired, not so forcefully as in *Les Tragiques* however, and most of the meditations end with the ecstatic contemplation of the divinity and the omnipotence of the Almighty.

As has been suggested in the analysis of the meditations, d'Aubigné is not as impartial as he would have us believe. The objects of his attack, the ingratitude of the King, the injustices inflicted on the Protestants etc., are familiar to readers of his epic poem and prose works. Although he does not mention the offenders personally there is present an obvious vindictive intent.

"The Meditations on the Psalms"

D'Aubigné has been criticized in "The Méditations"[7] for having followed the texts of the psalms too closely, for abandoning lyricism in favor of commentary, for being too didactic and discursive and not impassioned, and not intent on creating an original work but a mere commentary. These remarks are to a large extent justified, but one can say in d'Aubigné's favor that the very personality of the man can be seen in them. He possessed a burning sense of dedication to truth, and it was not possible for him to conceive of trifling with the word of God. His aim was to convey to the reader the richness of Holy Scripture, and in this he succeeded. Today we can regret that the meditations be so didactic but we cannot fail to admire the erudition of their author. Finally, it is symptomatic of the author's own creative process that in writing the meditations he placed himself in the position of a contemporary psalmist with the advantage of hindsight, and sought to rewrite the psalm in the biblical style of the original, yet including the fruits of his reading, his experience and knowledge of textual exegesis. "The Meditations" can still be read as a literary work with a continuing theological significance.

CHAPTER 8

A Poet of Many Parts

I *Religious Verse*

NEAR the end of his life, in 1630, d'Aubigné published the *Petites oeuvres meslées,* which included a collection of religious verse.[1] The first part comprises a number of poems in *vers mesurés,* the fashion for which had been spread by Antoine de Baïf. D'Aubigné appears to have experimented in this form to vie with his acquaintances, the Catholic Nicolas Rapin and the Protestant Odet de La Noue. In the tenth letter of the *Lettres sur diverses sciences* and the preface to the collection, he mentions the difficulties he had encountered in composing such verse. The main obstacle, he claims, in writing *vers mesurés* in French is that there is no tonic accent, so that there are three pyrrhic feet (that is, six short syllables) for every spondee (that is, two long syllables). Although such quantitative verse in French lacks grace when read or spoken, it improves greatly when it has a musical setting, especially when the setting is provided by such an accomplished musician as Claude Le Jeune who had composed music for a psalm heard by d'Aubigné at a concert given in his honor in Paris. The rendering of the psalm greatly impressed our author.

Figuring in the collection are twelve psalms, a grace and thanksgiving prayer, the *Nunc dimittis,* the *Te deum,* and a poem entitled "Larmes pour Suzanne de Lezai, espouse de l'auteur," which is in rhyming octosyllabics but placed here at the poet's request so as to follow Psalm 88. The poems no doubt represent d'Aubigné's favorite liturgical pieces, for he has used five of the six psalms which provided the basis of "The Meditations," and canticles and prayers which were the most commonly employed.

The majority of the *vers mesurés* are in rhyme and the language is simple; the result is interesting, if not particularly memorable. If a comparison is made between d'Aubigné's paraphrases and the text of the Geneva Bible which preceded "The Meditations," it transpires that on occasions he makes little change. For example, in the opening lines of Psalm 16 the Geneva Bible has "Garde-moi, O Dieu fort: car je me suis retiré vers toi. O mon ame, tu as dit à l'Eternel: Tu es le Seigneur, mon bien ne vient point jusqu'à toi." The corresponding passage by d'Aubigné reads:

> Dieu fort, garde moi qui tousjours me suis mis,
> Et tousjours retiré dessous ta bonté.
> Ma pauvre ame, tu as dit à l'Eternel:
> Tout mon bien ne peut estre haussé vers toi.

Preserve me, Oh God: for in thee do I put my trust. Oh my soul, thou hast said unto the Lord, Thou art my Lord: my goodness extendeth not to thee.

D'Aubigné sometimes tries to experiment with the meter so as to improve the effect, as in his paraphrase of Psalm 133, where he seeks to recapture the light tone of the original by using short lines. The Geneva Bible reads "Voici, o que c'est chose bonne, et que c'est chose plaisante, que freres s'entretiennent, mesmes ensemble," which corresponds to d'Aubigné's version:

> Voici le plaisir
> Entier et parfait,
> C'est de voir en paix
> Freres et voisins
> Tous biens accordés
> S'esgayer entr'eux.

Behold, how good and how pleasant it is for brethren to dwell together in unity!

It might be possible to criticize his version on the grounds that it lacks the gravity and majestic tone of the psalmic original, and yet d'Aubigné does follow the spirit and the letter of the original very closely. In spite of an occasional tendency to elaborate in his paraphrases, the main aim of the poet was to remain as detached as possible from the task in hand. In *Les Tragiques* he felt more at liberty to produce a poetry which revealed his own religious viewpoint; but in the psalms he was dealing with a sacred text and hence he felt the necessity for his detachment.

The relatively small proportion of *vers mesurés* in d'Aubigné's work underlines the experimental nature of the form and the author's constant preoccupation with new genres and styles.

II "L'Hiver"

Introducing the second part of the collection is a poem "L'Hiver," which, as the poet explains, is an allusion to the skylark emigrating for the winter, just as lascivious desires leave a man as he enters old age. The very title of the group of poems is intended to form a contrast with d'Aubigné's earlier collection, *Le Printemps,* concerned with profane love. "L'Hiver" is thus the poem of an elderly man ashamed of the follies of his youth. In the alexandrines of the six-lined strophes he proclaims his love of the winter season: "J'aime l'hyver, qui vient purger mon coeur du vice,/ Comme de peste l'air, la terre de serpens" (*P,* ll.11-12) ("I like the winter which comes to purge my heart of vice, as it does the air of plague and the earth of serpents"). He looks forward to death: "Mais la mort n'est pas loin: cette mort est suivie/D'un vivre sans mourir, fin d'une fausse vie" (*P,* ll.31-32) ("But death is not far away: this death is followed by a life without death, it is the end of a false life"); and to renewed religious awakening. After such an introduction, it is not surprising to find a number of poems of religious inspiration and orientation, ranging from a morning prayer to an octave on peace. The poems betray the poet's deep faith in, and submission to, God; the morning and evening prayers develop in heterometric lines, conceits which are current throughout d'Aubigné's writing. In the former he concludes with the paradox that through death the Christian finds life, and in the latter there is an appeal to find peace in faith and an attack on the weak-willed and the hesitant, with the poet asking God to ensure that he is not seduced by the "paraître":

> Delivre nous des vains mensonges,
> Et des illusions des foibles en la foi:
> Que le corps dorme en paix, que l'esprit veille à toi,
>   Pour ne veiller à songes.

(*P,* ll.5-8)

Deliver us from vain lies and from the illusions of the fainthearted: may the body sleep in peace and the mind attend to you so as not to attend to dreams.

The poet's sense of personal sin is manifest in his "Prayer and Confession," where we catch a glimpse of his turbulent past as he confesses: "Mes yeux de mes desirs corrupteurs ont cerché/ L'horreur, mes mains le sang, et mon coeur les vengeances" (*P*, ll.5-6) ("My eyes with my corrupting desires have looked for horror, my hands for blood and my heart for revenge"). There appears too his sense of having been persecuted for the faith: "La langue du meschant deschire mon honneur,/Quand de plume et de voix le tien j'escris et chante" (*P*, ll.37-38). ("The tongue of the wicked tears my honor to pieces, when I write and sing of yours with my pen and voice"). In a prayer composed by the author when a prisoner of war and condemned to death, there is a poignant, plaintive note as he reiterates his complete submission to the will of God:

> Je veux que mon ame suive,
> Ou soit libre, ou soit captive,
> Tes plaisirs: rien ne me chaut;
> Tout plaist pourveu qu'il te plaise,
> O Dieu, pour me donner l'aise,
> Donne-moi ce qu'il me faut.

(*P*, ll.7-12)

I want my soul to follow your pleasures whether it be free or captive: nothing matters to me; everything pleases me if it pleases you, Oh God, to give me comfort, give me what I need.

The reader is struck in such lines by the reserved tone of the poet's language; in these prayers destined for general use, d'Aubigné employs a nonemphatic style but one which at times can border on the precious. An example of this is to be found in the morning prayer, where the sun is personified and compared to Christ. The sun's face is only hidden from us by the earth's odious vapors and, by analogy:

> Jesus est toujours clair, mais lors son beau visage
> Nous cache ses rayons si doux,

> Quand nos pechez fumans entre le Ciel et nous,
> De vices redoublez enlevent un nuage
> Qui noircit le Ciel de courroux.
>
> (*P,* ll.11-15)

Jesus is always light, but then his beautiful face hides its such sweet rays from us, when our steaming sins raise between heaven and us a cloud of increased vices which causes the heavens to blacken with anger.

Stylistically there is little to distinguish these poems from the countless others written on religious themes by d'Aubigné's contemporaries. What is important is the force of the author's spiritual sincerity which here, as throughout his work, is so emphatically manifest.

III *"La Création"*

One of the lesser-known works by d'Aubigné is his long poem in fifteen cantos, "La Création." Written in Geneva at the end of his life, it may have been intended for his son Nathan,[3] but the poem was not pubished before the nineteenth century. Others had composed lengthy works about the creation, but it was above all Guillaume du Bartas who, by publishing *La Semaine* in 1578 and the *Seconde Semaine* in 1584, greatly influenced d'Aubigné. The author set out in "La Création" to show: "Qu'il est un Souverain, un Dieu lequel preside/Sur tout, et qui d'un frain droyturier ce tout guyde" (*CR,* 328) ("That there is a sovereign, a God which presides over everything, and with a just check guides the whole world"). The fifteen cantos offer a paean to the glory of God and His creation. The argument is drawn from Genesis and expounded with great respect for Calvinist doctrine. The didactic nature of the poem is overpowering, and the work is too long for d'Aubigné's terms of reference, for it develops into a quasi-scientific and humanist treatise on the nature of man and nature itself. The tendency toward prolixity, already evident in *Les Tragiques,* is even more marked. The eternity and power of God, the creation of light and air, the immensity of the heavens, the separation of the waters, the earth and its minerals, its trees, plants, and herbs, etc., are examined in some detail, often to the great detriment of the poetry. In describing the anatomy of man, for example, d'Aubigné presents us with an almost clinical description of the arm:

> Pour estendre et ployer le coude en general,
> Quatre muscles il a, l'un dict le brachial,
> Et l'autre le biceps, tous deux à son ply tendent,
> Les muscles longs et courts au contrayre l'estendent.
>
> (*CR*, 424)

To stretch and bend his elbow he has, in general, four muscles, one is called the brachial and the other the biceps, both are braced when you bend it, and, on the contrary, the long and short muscles allow you to extend it.

Although interesting as a work giving a panorama of Protestant and humanist views on divine foresight and as a confirmation of belief in the omniscience and bounty of the Almighty, the poem is a great disappointment as a work of art. In most ways the relative oblivion that surrounds it is justified.

IV Conclusion

In his production of verse on purely religious themes, d'Aubigné appears to have been restricted by his desire to write poetry in plain language, so as to allow the message to be understood more easily and so as not to interfere personally with the revelation of divine truth. He is far more impressive in productions of a more personal nature, where he can give full vent to his invective and allow his forceful personality a free rein.

V Verses Written on the Death of Jodelle

The *Vers funebres de Th. A. d'Aubigné, Gentilhomme Xantangeois, sur la mort d'Estienne Jodelle Parisien Prince des Poëtes Tragiques* appeared as a small plaquette in 1574.[4] D'Aubigné was one of the rare poets to bewail the death of Jodelle, who died in poverty, and the collection, comprising an ode, five sonnets, and a quatrain, points to the admiration that the young d'Aubigné had for his elder.[5] As is normal in literary "tombeaux" of this sort, the poems are eulogious. The eulogy is combined however with a certain social satire, for Jodelle, in spite of his greatness, was left to die forsaken and penniless:

> Jodelle est mort de pauvreté;
> La pauvreté a eu puissance
> Sur la richesse de la France....
>
> (*V*, ll.57-59)

Jodelle died of poverty; poverty had power over the richness of France.

Jodelle finds Hell more attractive than Paris, and complains of the injustice of his royal patrons: "Se plaint qu'il a esté la gloire de noz Rois,/Et que noz Rois n'ont peu cognoistre leur Jodelle" (*V*, Sonnet III, ll.3-4) ("He complains that he was the glory of our kings, and that our kings could not recognize their Jodelle"). The influence of the Pléiade is evident in the verses, and the poet repeats the Pléiade commonplaces of immortality through art, the importance of poetic fury, and the use of classical simile, etc. At the same time we see emerging d'Aubigné's tendency to interpret contemporary events in the light of divine judgment. Who can wonder at contemporary disorders for:

> Siècle malheureux et maudit,
> Où Mammon pour seul Dieu s'adore:
> Siècle plus miserable encore
> Cent mille fois que je n'ay dit:
> La noblesse demeure serve
> Soubz le populaire ennobly;
> Noz services sont en oubly:
> Les pourceaux enseignent Minerve.
>
> (*V*, ode, ll.49-56)

Unfortunate and cursed century, where Mammon is adored as only God: Oh century a hundred thousand times more wretched than I have said: the nobility remains a serf beneath the ennobled populace; our services are forgotten, the pigs teach Minerva.

VI *Poésies Diverses*

This miscellany of youthful verse assembled by Réaume and Caussade[6] shows how open d'Aubigné was to contemporary literary influences. The poems could have been penned by any of the multitude of poetasters composing in the 1570s and the previous decade. Written when he was only sixteen years of age, one poem (*PD*, 207) records the poet's great admiration for the prince of poets, Ronsard, whose influence over the poets of the second half of the sixteenth century was so great. D'Aubigné's debt to Petrarchist conceits and stylization is visible in his *Odes* to Diane (*PD,* 208, 212), as well as in the majority of the twenty-one sonnets. The traditional vocabulary of "ardeur, soupirs, douleurs, cruauté, etc." is well utilized, and there is often a wordplay in the hope of creating an emotional effect, as in "Ma paine me sera un doux contentement/Faisant plus douce fin que doux commencement" (*PD,* 210) ("My pain will be a sweet contentment for me, making a sweeter end than a sweet beginning"); and antithesis is in full evidence: "Faut-il qu'estant de feu tu soys toute de glace?" (*PD,* 250).

Such poems lack the personal twist given to the sonnets in *Le Printemps* and lack much of the author's characteristic dynamism. Although part of the Petrarchist convention, the theme of death is given here perhaps greater prominence than in other contemporary poets, and d'Aubigné comes back to it with amazing frequency. In one sonnet, he exclaims:

> Mais si le faux destain ne veut que je possede
> Le comble de mon heur, j'ay la mort seur remede
> Pour estaindre mon mal, mes desirs et mes veux.
>
> (*PD,* 250)

But if false destiny does not want me to possess the height of my happiness, I have death as a certain remedy to extinguish my suffering, my desires, and my wishes.

Inspired by Ovid's *Heroïdes,* as was Marot in his *Epistre de Maguelonne,* d'Aubigné reconstructed the lament of a girl deserted by her lover (*PD,* 215-219). The pathetic nature of the tale is highlighted when the young mother reacts to her father's wish to see the child abandoned in the forest: "Faut-il que vive encor la moytié de mon ventre/Dans le ventre afamé des fieres bestes entre?" (*PD,* 218) ("Must half of my belly, still alive, enter into the starving belly of wild animals?").

The shade of Ronsard looms large in a number of the elegies, whether it be in the autobiographical elegy, the *Poème de l'inconstance, Constance-Inconstance,* or *La Sorcière.* The use of fable and classical allusion is well in evidence and bears witness to a young d'Aubigné aspiring to imitate the Pléiade. In the elegy narrating his life, we find a number of themes which occur throughout his major works. His attitude toward the state of religion then prevalent is that true religion has been banished: "L'atheisme trompeur a chassé de son lieu/La pieté trop rude et la crainte de Dieu" (*PD,* 219) ("Deceiving atheism has chased from its position too austere piety and the fear of God"). He is convinced that he has been a victim of Fortune (*PD,* 220) and he regrets his riotous time in the infantry:

> Parmy des gens de pied cinq ou six ans entiers
> J'apprins des enragez les dangereux mestiers
> Et à n'avoir discours que de jeuz, de querelles,
> De bourdeaux, de putains, verolles, maquerelles,
> Renier Dieu de grace et braver de bel aer,
> Mespriser tout le monde, arrogamment parler.
>
> (*PD,* 221)

Among the infantry for five or six whole years I learned the dangerous tasks of the fanatics and to speak only of gambling, quarrels, pleasure houses, whores, the pox, "couplers," to deny God with grace and to brag debonairly, to pour scorn on everyone, to speak with arrogance.

God caused the poet to be wounded and thereby find Him (*PD,* 221). He denounces the materialism of his age and the jealousy the princes felt for him, affirming that he had always acted sincerely and fairly with them. With great venom, he attacks those responsible for the harsh treatment he considers he has received, and which no doubt accounts for the bitterness of the poet during the last years of his life:

> Mes services perduz, ma jeunesse trompee,
> Mon sang perdu, ma peau dix et sept fois coupee,
> Mes Etatz possedez et jamais pretenduz,
> Un pré, une maison et trois moulins vendus,
> La haine des plus Grans pour ceux qui me haïssent,
> Les trahistres, les ingratz que j'aime me trahissent.
>
> (*PD,* 224)

My services wasted, my youth deceived, my blood spilled, my skin lacerated seventeen times, my estates occupied and never claimed, a meadow, a house, and three mills sold, the hatred of the mighty on account of those who hate me, the traitors and those ungrateful people that I love betray me.

He concludes with a complete and utter condemnation of the princes: "Les Princes n'ont de moy memoire, ny moy d'eux" (*PD,* 225).

Such declarations help to throw more light on the life and the inventiveness of the poet who never ceases to astound by the very variety of his output.

VII Discours par stances avec l'esprit du feu Roy Henry Quatriesme

A résumé of the poet's attitude toward Henry IV is to be found in the *Discours par stances*.[7] In the six-lined stanzas in alexandrines and by the use of rather esoteric allusions, he repeats his admiration of the king and his criticism of his policies. His admiration dates from the time when, as a Protestant prince, Henri, like Caesar, came, saw, and conquered. D'Aubigné reminds the reader how, divinely inspired, he foresaw that the king would be assassinated when he betrayed God with his heart. Ravaillac, "l'infame poux, le ver qui mit ce Roy par terre' (*Di,* 1.52), had been sent by God to commit the act. The king is accused of having sacrificed God for his own temporal ends and of having suppressed learning and honesty: "Dessoubs toy n'a fleury le docte et sa science:/Tu as hay la ferme et droicte conscience (*Di,* 11.97-98) ("Beneath you the learned man and his knowledge have not flourished; you have hated the firm and upright mind"). Thinking of his own harsh treatment at the hands of the king, he claims that Henry distributed "Les honneurs aux vaincus et la honte au vainqueur" (*Di,* 1.114), persecuted the faithful, and curried the favor of Rome. As in *Misères* he is particularly vociferous against the "enfans de Loyolle," "la troupe qui ment Jesus au bout des langues," for the Jesuits were a great thorn in the flesh of this old Huguenot warrior and the constant butt of his attacks.

From Henry IV, d'Aubigné then turns to the young Louis XIII, the child king, who sits "sur la peau de [son] pere." He is warned against those who try and distort the memory of his father and those who plot against his life. He is in danger from the influence of Rome and the Catholic church. The monarchy is a natural state and reflects God's will, but the king who allows himself to be subjected to others is not worthy of his position (*Di,* 11.331-33).

Marie de Medici, the queen mother, is equally the object of the author's mordant invective, for she is encouraged to forget the evil ways of Florence and respect the needs of France. In an "apophetie," probably induced by the queen's conflict with her son, he foresees her ruin.

The *Discours par stances* can be compared to *Les Tragiques,* with its forceful attack on the princes: d'Aubigné is bitter in his criticism of Henry IV, the Roman Catholic church and what he sees as the obnoxious Italian influence of the Medicis. It can also be seen as a poetic expression of many of d'Aubigné's ideas concerning the monarchy, such as are evident in his prose work, *Du Devoir mutuel des Roys et des subjects.* At times the allusions are difficult to comprehend and somewhat sibylline for a modern reader. We must not forget that d'Aubigné's view of the world was a highly personal and stylized one. In this poem as in others, he reproduces his thought after having digested all the facts: he does not feel the need to explain and justify, he is convinced of his own truth and sincerity. It suggests that his mind worked on an elevated plane, full of imagery, and that he interpreted the world through the eyes of the psalmist. Although we may accuse him of obscurity, he surely compels our admiration for his continuous and dogged reaffirmation of his belief in his own analysis of events.

VIII "Sonnets et pièces épigrammatiques"

Among the Tronchin manuscripts, Réaume and Caussade found and collected together a number of satirical poems in a variety of metres which, in the style of the late sixteenth-century satirists, criticized vices both in general and in the particular.[8] There are twenty-three epigrammatic sonnets and fifty-six others of differing length, ranging from the epigrammatic quatrain to a work of 168 lines in six-lined stanzas, entitled the *Prudents.* To these may be added the *Tombeaux du style de Sainct Innocent,* so named because it was possible to commission epitaphs from professional writers who took orders in the St. Innocent cemetery. This latter work contains twelve epigrammatic epitaphs.[9]

Many of these poems form a poetic background to d'Aubigné's other literary output. They exploit points touched upon elsewhere, whether it be in *Les Tragiques,* the *Confession du Sieur de Sancy,* or the more austere political pamphlets.

The central theme of *Misères* — France torn apart by two warring children — is echoed in the second sonnet:

> La France alaicte encor deux enfans aujourd'huy,
> Dont l'un à ses deux mains tient les bouts de sa mere,
> Et à grands coups de pied veut empescher son frere
> D'avoir sa nourriture aussi bien que luy....

France still suckles two children today of whom one clings to his mother's breasts with both hands and wants to prevent his brother with great kicks from sharing his food....

In Sonnet X, he refers to Charles IX in terms reminiscent of those employed for Henry III in *Princes:* "Sardanapale n'eust de masle qu'une image,/Et de femme l'esprit, le vouloir et les faicts..." ("Sardanapalus only had an appearance of a male, and the mind, the will, and the deeds of a woman..."). Elsewhere, a sentence in prose taken from the dedication by Sancy of his *Confession* to the Cardinal du Perron, is made into a stanza of a poem directed against papal interference with the sovereignty of the French king: "Il me souvient aussi, que le Roy vous ayant un jour commandé de prouver par discours la Divinité, vous ravistes les Dames en admiration et vous offristes quant et quant à la preuve de l'*antiphaticque,* ce qui eust esté plaisant, mais le Roy vous fit taire" (*C,* 575-76) ("I remember too that the king, having ordered you one day to prove the existence of God by reason, you amazed the women and at the same time you proposed the proof of the 'antifatica,' which would have been pleasing, but the king bade you fall silent"). This is rendered as follows:

> Au front de Henry troisiesme
> Un jour il prit en probleme
> A prouver la Deité,
> Pour s'offrir à la replicque
> Il prenoit l'antifaticque
> Quand il en fut arresté.
>
> (*PE,* X)

In front of Henry III one day he undertook the task of proving the deity, to propose a reply he was going to take the "antifatica" when he was prevented.

A number of poems reflect a certain preciosity and can be linked with the poet's stay in the royal courts of Navarre. The theme of such sonnets is the eternal one of love and d'Aubigné seems to be following convention rather than natural inclination for his inspiration. One poem which probably would have earned him praise at court for its wit and invention is the sonnet in which he compares his friendship with his beloved with the card game of "Prime," calling upon the precise terms for the various aspects of their association:

> Ton baiser est le *vade,* encor que je l'estime
> Le comble de mon heur, les *envis* sont tes yeux,
> Le *renvy* est ton sein, et qui veult avoir mieux,
> Le *reste* ne se peut abandonner sans crime.
>
> (*PE,* sonnet, XIII)

D'Aubigné's characteristic venom will out, however, and in one sonnet his vituperation turns against Charles IX's counselors, whom he blames for the evil which has befallen France:

> Le conseiller, le noble et le peuple et l'Eglise
> Corrompus, mutinés, irritez, vicieux,
> Ont mesprisé le droict, l'honneur, la loy, les Cieux
> Par l'or, le fer, le meurtre et l'avare Prestrise.
>
> (*PE,* sonnet, XV)

The counselor, the nobleman, the people, and the Church are corrupt, in revolt, irritable, and full of vice, they have scorned what is right, honor, justice, and heaven through gold, the sword, murder, and the miserliness of its priests.

In another, he suggests that heaven is irritated by the sight of so much injustice:

> Il ne peut plus souffrir les meurtres des germains,
> Les rouges cruautez et la poizon traistresse,
> L'inceste et le peché que sa main vengeresse
> Punit des mesmes feux qui ne sont pas esteints.
>
> (*PE,* sonnet, XIX)

It can no longer suffer the slaughter of brothers, the blood-red cruelties and the treacherous poison, the incest, and the sin that its avenging hand punishes with those same fires which have not been extinguished.

A curious mixture of deep religious conviction and Gallic salt is displayed especially in the "Pièces épigrammatiques." We tend to forget nowadays the earnest desire of sixteenth-century satirists to discredit their adversaries with some mordant comment about their morality. As we have mentioned before, it was customary to level accusations of the most heinous crimes against those in authority: sodomy, incest, prostitution, etc., are mentioned with wearying frequency. A monk is referred to as a "filz de putain" (*PE,* IV), the opponents to the "Fermes" are "suppostes de l'Enfer" (*PE,* IX), Mary Stuart is not "plus chaste qu'une putain" (*PE,* XIX). Puns which we would consider of doubtful taste are numerous. Some are similar to those used by Rabelais, as for example when d'Aubigné criticizes the influence Father Cotton has over the king:

> Sire, vostre humeur n'est pareille
> Aux autres Roys qui ont vescu:
> Le Cotton vous bouche l'oreille,
> Il leur servoit de torche cu.
>
> (*PE,* XX)

Sire, your condition is not like that of other kings who have lived: the cotton blocks up your ears, it was an arse-wiper for them.

The invective reaches its most sickening intensity in a poem directed against the dogma of transubstantiation. The argument advanced is that if bread and wine are transformed into Christ's body and blood then they enter the priest's body as such. The logical conclusion of this situation for d'Aubigné is that:

> Tout ce que tient le Prestre en sa poche, en sa manche,
> En sa braguette est sainct et de plus je vous dy
> Qu'en aiant desjeuné de son Dieu le dimanche,
> Vous devez adorer son estron du lundy.
>
> (*PE,* XXVII)

Everything that a priest holds in his pocket, in his sleeve, in his codpiece is sacred, and furthermore, I tell you that having lunched on his God on Sunday, you ought to adore the stool on Monday.

Nevertheless, d'Aubigné certainly possessed wit and versatility. His sonnets, if they lack the luster of the best poetry, do lead up to powerful epigrammatic conclusions. He also had mastered the art of being amusing at the expense of others and was able to turn it to the benefit of his cause. His comment on the death of a monk who drowned in the latrines at Maillezais well illustrates this point:

> S'il est dit que chacun se perde
> Dedans le champ de son mestier,
> Meure au combat le Chevalier
> Et le pourceau dedans la merde.
>
> (*PE,* Tombeaux, II)

If it is said that everyone should die within the field of his own trade, may the knight die in battle and the pig within the excrement.

The satire is not always quite so scurrilous and can be subtle, recalling to mind Du Bellay rather than L'Estoile's *Journal. Sur l'Apotheose du Cardinal Boromé* is one such example. The octosyllabic six-lined stanzas all end with a reference to Borromée and have a refreshing satirical yet rythmic lightness about them:

> Aux devotions coustumieres,
> Aux serments, aux voeux, aux prieres
> Christ est mort, Dieu n'est pas nommé;
> Sans plus en Italie on parle
> De la Madone et de Sainct Charle,
> D'elle moins que de Boromé.
>
> (*PE,* XXIV)

In the usual devotions, oaths, vows, and prayers, Christ is dead, God is not named without in Italy people speaking of the Madonna and St. Charles and, of her, less than of Borromée.

These manifestations of d'Aubigné's wit remind us of the doubtless daunting verbal pyrotechnics he was able to provide at the least provocation. The poems have become dated because of their allusions to contemporary events, but they allow us to realize that d'Aubigné must have been feared by his antagonists not just for his sword but also for his pen and his tongue.

In this collection, as in the medley of others that we have considered in this chapter, d'Aubigné shows himself to have been a versatile and daring poet, if not always a good one. He feared nobody but God, and his need for constant movement led him to be always on the *qui-vive,* an ever vigilant guardian of his cause, and to be ceaselessly in search of new ways of exercising his literary talents and native wit.

CHAPTER 9

Conclusion

SEEKING d'Aubigné's characteristics as revealed in the preceding pages, it becomes obvious that he was a man of varied talents. His literary output was relatively prolific and diverse; he tried his hand at poetry, religious and profane, epic and epigrammatic; he wrote a history, pamphlets, a novel, political treatises, and learned meditations on the Psalms. He was also an avid correspondent, writing letters to his contemporaries in positions of authority. He was as formidable a warrior with the sword as with the pen, and he played a leading role in the Wars of Religion and the Protestant-Catholic skirmishes under Henri IV and during the regency of the young Louis XIII. Even while in forced retirement in Geneva, he set himself up as a military adviser and offered his services to other Swiss cantons and to the Maréchal de Lesdiguières. He would appear to have been a man of great strength of character and energy, easily offended and always ready to defend his point of view. Neither afraid of authority, nor reticent to criticize, he guarded jealously his own beliefs. Such a man commands our respect. Never once do we find him doubting his Protestant position, never once does he entertain the idea that he could possibly be wrong. There was only one true religion and that was the one practiced by the Reformed church. His intransigent attitude did not escape censure from members of his own church, but this did nothing to make him modify his opinions. Society has always produced a few men of the moral caliber of d'Aubigné, men who have been prepared to stake their life on what they believe.

As a man of letters he stands out from his contemporaries, belonging as he does more to the sixteenth century by his temperament and style than to the seventeenth. It is highly significant that much of his work remained unpublished at the time of his death. Some of it was politically too explosive to have appeared when it

Conclusion

was written, other works were purposefully withheld, for example *Le Printemps,* for personal reasons. *Les Tragiques* was published too late to arouse the now fairly complacent Protestants, and the language of the poem appeared archaic to many readers. The *Faeneste* enjoyed a moderate success and had a certain topical piquancy about it. But in this, as in most of the author's literary production, the quality of the inspiration and the expression is often marred by the sheer weight of the emotional impact. As some authors do not have a sense of the ridiculous, so d'Aubigné did not realize the dangers of excess. Although it may be possible to attribute such proliferation of detail and example to the very force of his own personality, the sad fact remains that today, instead of being crushed by the overpowering strength of the arguments, we tend, because of our intellectual detachment, to find them wearisome.

And yet this very enthusiasm on the part of d'Aubigné is his strength as well as his weakness. His work is at first difficult of access. It needs careful study to appreciate the references to historical and contemporary religious events, to understand the scholarly allusions of a polyglot humanist. Nonetheless, the man possessed a style and a conception of life which merit our attention and which help us to understand the troubled times in which he lived. His work also has a more than historical value, for it raises the eternal problems of the conflict between good and evil, between justice and injustice, and the interpretation that can be given to events when divine ordinance is believed to control the life of man. D'Aubigné is a difficult author, sometimes an obscure one, but also — as we hope this study will have established — a very worthwhile one.

Notes and References

Chapter One

1. Collection Tronchin, Geneva, Bibliothèque Publique et Universitaire, Vols. 151-161.
2. See *Lettres d'affaires personnelles,* in *Oeuvres complètes,* edited by E. Réaume and F. de Caussade (Paris: A. Lemerre), vol. 1, p. 325. See also Letter XXV.
3. See *Oeuvres,* edited by H. Weber, J. Bailbé, and M. Soulié (Paris: Gallimard), p. 871.

Chapter Two

1. *Sa Vie à ses enfants,* in Weber edition, pp. 381-463.
2. *Poesies diverses,* p. 208; hereafter cited as *PD* in the text; all references, unless otherwise indicated are to page numbers in the Réaume and Caussade edition, vol. 3. References to *Le Printemps* are preceded by *PR* with the appropriate line, sonnet, ode, stance number. They are taken from: *Le Printemps: Stances et Odes,* edited by F. Desonay (Geneva: Droz, 1952).
3. See Jacques Pineaux, *La Poésie des Protestants de langue française (1559-1598)* (Paris, Klincksieck, 1971), p. 57.
4. See his praise of Ronsard and his acknowledgment of his debt toward him: "C'est luy qui a coupé le filet que la France avoit soubs la langue" (Lettre XI, *Oeuvres,* p. 860).
5. See the notes to H. Weber's critical edition.
6. S. Rocheblave: *La Vie d'un héros: Agrippa d'Aubigné* (Paris: Hachette, 1912), p. 53f.
7. See Glauco Natoli, "Il *Printemps* di d'Aubigné," in his book, *Figure e problemi della cultura francese* (Florence, 1956), pp. 43-82.
8. See. A.-M. Schmidt's essay on d'Aubigné in his edition of *Les Baroques: Th. A. d'Aubigné: Oeuvres lyriques* (Paris: Mazenod, 1963), pp. 245-54.
9. See my article "Montaigne and the Mask," *L'Esprit Créateur* 8, no. 3 (1968), 198-207.
10. See the notes to accompany the critical editions prepared by H. Weber and B. Gagnebin.

11. See *Le Printemps: Stances et Odes,* ed. F. Desonay (Geneva: Droz, 1952).

12. See E. Droz, "La Reine Marguerite de Navarre et la vie littéraire à la Cour de Nérac (1579-1582)," *Bulletin de la Société des Bibliophiles de Guyenne* 80 (1964), 77-120.

13. See A. Paraillous, "Agrippa d'Aubigné et l'Agenais," *Revue de l'Agenais* 95 (1969), 295-305.

14. *Oeuvres complètes,* ed. Réaume, I, p. 532.

15. See the Desonay edition, p. viii.

16. See G. Natoli; Floyd Gray, "Variation on a Renaissance Theme: The Poetic landscape and a *Stance* of A. d'Aubigné," *Philological Quarterly* 44 (1965), 433-44; W. Drost, "Petrarchismo e realismo nella poesia di d'Aubigné giovane," *Rivista di letterature moderne e comparate* 15, no. 3 (1962) 165-87; M. Jeanneret, "Les Styles d'Agrippa d'Aubigné," *Studi Francesi* 11 (1967), 246-57; R. Griffin, "Agrippa d'Aubigné's *Le Printemps* and early French Baroque poetry," *Symposium* 19 (1965), 197-213.

17. See W. Drost, p. 175.

18. See the introduction to Hierosme d'Avost, *Essais sur les sonnets du divin Petrarque,* ed. K. C. Cameron and M. V. Constable (University of Exeter, 1974).

19. F. Gray, p. 441.

20. See E. Droz, p. 106.

21. See ode 13.

22. See introduction, Desonay edition, pp. xxviii-xxix.

23. See A. Guillaume, "Le *Printemps* du sieur d'Aubigné," *La Nouvelle Revue Critique* 50 (1933) 1-16, especially p. 14.

Chapter Three

1. See *Sa Vie à ses enfants,* ed. Weber, p. 405. The concept of the poem can be placed several years earlier, in 1572, when after being wounded in a fracas at a hotel in the Beauce, d'Aubigné took refuge at the Château de Talcy. During the state of concussion which followed the accident, d'Aubigné is said to have had a vision which formed the basis of his poem. See Jacques Bailbé, *Agrippa d'Aubigné: Poète des Tragiques* (Caen: Université de Caen, 1968), pp. xxxv f.

2. *Les Tragiques,* Weber edition, *Aux lecteurs,* p. 4; hereafter cited as *T;* the Books of *Les Tragiques* are designated by roman numerals.

3. See A. Garnier, II, 181-245.

4. R. L. Regosin has made a study of the close relationship between his style and that of the apocalypse in *The Poetry of Inspiration: Agrippa d'Aubigné's Les Tragiques*, University of North Carolina, Studies in the Romance languages and literatures, no. 88, (Chapel Hill: University of North Carolina Press, 1970).

5. In Agrippa d'Aubigné, *Les Tragiques,* ed. I. D. McFarlane (London: Athlone Press, 1970), p. 31.
6. In Réaume and Caussade edition, II, 226–31.
7. It is of interest on this topic to compare the emotional satirical portrait of Henry III in *Princes* with the few comparatively civil lines in the *Histoire universelle:*

Prince d'agreable conversation avec les siens, amateur des lettres, liberal par delà tous les Rois, courageux en jeunesse, et lors desiré de tous; en vieillesse aimé de peu, qui avoit de grandes parties de Roi, souhaité pour l'estre avant qu'il le fust, et digne du Royaume s'il n'eust point regné; c'est ce qu'on peut dire un bon François" (Maillé, 1620), III, 183.

8. *Oeuvres complètes,* ed. Cohen, II, 1009.
9. T. M. Greene, *The Descent from Heaven. A study in epic continuity* (New Haven: Yale University Press, 1963).
10. Chassanion de Monistrol, *Des Grands et Redoutables Jugemens et Punitions de Dieu* (Morges: Jean le Preux, 1581).
11. See my article, "Henri III — the Antichristian King," *Journal of European Studies* 4 (1974), 152–63.
12. This view had already been expressed by Chassanion de Monistrol, Book I, p. 3.

Tous les maux sont si communs et si frequens aujourd'hui entre les hommes, qu'il semble vrayement que ce ne soit qu'une mer de monstres hideux de ce monde-ci, ou une forest espesse pleine de brigans et voleurs, ou quelque desert horrible, auquel les habitants de la terre devenus sauvages et desnaturez, hors de leurs sens et raison humaine, sont transformez en bestes brutes: les uns semblables à des tigres ou des lions, les autres à des loups, les autres à des renars, les autres à des chiens et porceaux.

13. See the studies by Bailbé, Buffum, Sauerwein, and Weber.
14. See L. Forster, *The Icy Fire* (Cambridge, 1969).
15. Cesare Ripa, *Iconology...,* trans. G. Richardson, (London, 1777–1779), Vol. II, Fig. 269, pp. 45–46.

Chapter Four

1. The *Avis aux lecteurs* preceding the second book implies that a separate edition of Book I had been published. See the Weber edition of *Oeuvres,* p. 1362, to which all quotations from the *Faeneste* refer; hereafter cited as *F.*
2. See H. Weber, "Structure et langage dans *Les Avantures du Baron de Faeneste", Mélanges ... P. Jourda* (Paris: Nizet, 1970), pp. 111–30; and Ian R. Morrison, "'Paraître' and 'Être': thoughts on d'Aubigné's

'Avantures du Baron de Faeneste,'" *Modern Language Review* 68 (1973), 762-70.
  3. H. Weber, p. 126.
  4. See A. Garnier, II, 44.
  5. H. Weber, *Oeuvres,* p. xli.
  6 See P. de Vaissière, *Gentilshommes Campagnards de l'Ancienne France* (Paris: Perrin, 1903), who devotes a chapter to "Les gentilshommes campagnards dans la littérature du XVIIe et du XVIIIe siècle," pp. 261-309. See pp. 296-97:

Les gentilshommes campagnards apparaissent aux yeux prevenus des courtisans, comme d'amusantes caricatures et de grotesques fantoches, qu'est-ce, lorsqu'à ces bonnes gens prend la fantaisie de s'aventurer hors de leur province et de venir étaler à la ville leur naïveté, leur rusticité, leur vantardise, leur vanité. Malheur à eux, car là les attendent les plus impitoyables quolibets, les plus sanglants affronts, les plus cruelles railleries.

  7. See *Sa Vie à ses enfants,* ed. Weber, p. 402:

Sur ce point estants commencez les amours dudit Roy et de la jeune Tignonville, qui tant qu'elle fut fille resista vertueusement, le Roy vouloit y employer Aubigné, ayant posé pour chose seure, que rien ne luy estoit impossible. Cestui-ci, assez vicieux en grandes choses, et qui peut-estre n'eust refusé ce service par caprice à un sien compagnon, se banda tellement contre le nom et l'effect de macquereau, qu'il nommoit vice de basace, que les caresses desmesurees de son Maistre, ou les infinies supplications, jusques à joindre les mains devant luy à genoux, ne le peurent esmouvoir.

  8. See J. Alter: *L'Esprit Antibourgeois sous l'Ancien Régime* (Geneva: Droz, 1970), II, 85.
  9. It is interesting to read the poetic works of Sonnet de Courval, one of d'Aubigné's contemporaries, who has left us with some excellent satirical vignettes of the Court of Louis XIII. See *Oeuvres poétiques de Courval Sonnet* (Paris: Prosper Blanchemain, 1876) 3 vols. See *Avis au lecteur,* I, 4:

...aucune passion ni affection particulière ne m'a poussé à traicter ce subject satyrique et mordant, que le seul zele de l'honneur de la France et le bien de l'Estat; car, voyant des moeurs si dépravées, des abus si évidents, un siècle si pervers et corrompu, siècle remply d'iniquité, tout noyé au desbord de ses vices, rocher endurcy en l'opiniastreté de ses erreurs, Afrique abondante en monstres de desordre et de confusion, il m'a esté comme impossible de me retrancher dans le silence, donner tresve à ma plume, faire banqueroute à mon devoir, retenir mes conceptions soubs bride, et empescher les saillies et boutades poëtiques de ma muse... *difficile est... satyram non scribere.*

10. See C. Lenient: *La Satire en France ou la littérature militante au XVIe siècle* (Paris: Hachette, 1886), II, 179.

11. The personification of abstract notions was widespread, as was the criticism of corruption and injustice. See Sonnet de Courval, *Avis au lecteur,* I, 5-6:

Si nous entrons dans les sacrez temples d'Astrée, dans les palais de Themis, nous trouverons que l'injustice et la corruption y sont en quartier et en très-grande authorité, la Justice à ressort rompu, toute courbée et pliée soubs le pesant faix de l'injustice, toute eschevelée, et à teste qui luy tombe sur les pieds, à front fait à sillons, à yeux ternis et enfoncez, à maschoire avalée, à cuir tout flestry, à teint jaunastre et plombé, à voix basse et cassée, à paroles entre-couppées de hocquets et fréquents soupirs, faisant ses tristes complaintes contre ses ministres et officiers, qui par concussion, rapines et chicaneries, l'ont ainsi desfigurée, et mise en si piteux estat qu'il ne luy reste aucune marque de son premier embonpoinct, gaillarde santé et ancienne dignité.

12. For an examination of the link between the two authors see J. Bailbé, "Rabelais et d'Aubigné," *Bibliothèque d'Humanisme et Renaissance,* 21 (1959), 380–419.

13. And yet in Book IV, chapter XIV is introduced for no apparent reason unless it be to continue the satire of Faeneste's attachment to genealogy already alluded to in Chapter VII.

14. See H. Weber: "Structure et langage dans *Les Avantures du Baron de Faeneste.*"

15. Ibid., p. 114.

16. See Bailbé's article.

17. S. Rocheblave, *Agrippa d'Aubigné* (Paris: Hachette, 1910), p. 160.

18. Jacques Bailbé: 'Quelques aspects du burlesque dans *Les Avantures du Baron de Faeneste* d'Agrippa d'Aubigné', *Mélanges ... R. Lebègue* (Paris: Nizet, 1969), pp. 135–45.

19. See G. Reynier, *Le Roman réaliste au XVIIe sicle* (Paris: Hachette, 1914), p. 74.

20. Ibid., pp. 77-78.

21. Ibid., pp. 88-89.

22. Th. Heyer, *Théodore-Agrippa d'Aubigné à Genève* (Genève: Ramboz et Schuchardt, 1870), p. 42.

23. Ibid.

24. Ibid.

25. 2 vols. (Cologne, 1729).
26. Ibid., p. 2.
27. *Les Avantures du Baron de Faeneste* (Paris: P. Jannet, 1855), p. ix.

Chapter Five

1. Weber edition, pp. 573-666, Réaume and Caussade, 233-373. Our references are to the Weber edition; hereafter cited as *C*.
2. See *Nouvelle biographie générale* (Paris: Hoefer/Didot, 1867); P. Villey, "La Confession de Sancy," *Revue d'Histoire litteraire de la France,* 22 (1915), 160-216; A. Garnier, *A. d'Aubigné et le parti protestant,* II, 245-68; A. Garnier, *A. d'Aubigné,* Chapter IV.
3. Weber edition, pp. 886-91.
4. It first appeared in the *Recueil de diverses pièces servant à l'histoire de Henry III* (1660). For the text see Réaume and Caussade, II, 653-84; hereafter cited as *D*.
5. See A. Garnier, III, 1-26. For the text see Réaume and Caussade, II, 71-109; hereafter cited *CA*. See also F. A. Clarke, *Huguenot warrior: The life and times of Henri de Rohan, 1579-1638* (The Hague: Nijhof, 1966), Chapter 2; P. Villey, "A propos du *Caducé* d'Agrippa d'Aubigné," in *Mélanges, offerts par ses amis et ses élèves à M. G. Lanson,* (Paris, 1922), pp. 154-61.

Chapter Six

1. See Weber edition, p. 1239.
2. A. Garnier, III, 116. The texts of the two treatises are to be found in Réaume and Caussade, II, 3-69. The *Debvoir mutuel* is included also in the Weber edition, pp. 465-89.
3. See also *Sa Vie à ses enfans,* Weber edition, p. 447.
4. See A. Garnier, III, 113-14.

Chapter Seven

1. See T. C. Cave, *Devotional poetry in France c. 1570-1613* (Cambridge: Cambridge University Press, 1969).
2. Ibid., p. 9.
3. See M. Jeanneret, *Poésie et tradition biblique au XVIe siècle* (Paris: Corti, 1969), pp. 400-17.
4. See Weber edition, p. 1251; hereafter the meditations will be cited as *M*.
5. Ibid., p. 1272.
6. See T. C. Cave, p. 29.
7. See M. Jeanneret.

Chapter Eight

1. For the text see the edition of Réaume and Caussade, III, 271-314; hereafter cited as *P*. For critical remarks about this collection see M. Jeanneret, *Poésie et tradition biblique au XVIe siècle,* pp. 251-69.

2. Numbers 3, 16, 51, 54, 73, 88, 110, 116, 121, 128, 133, 143. Réaume and Caussade have also included three love poems from an earlier period.

3. See A.-M. Schmidt, *La Poésie Scientifique en France au Seizième Siècle* (Paris: A. Michel, 1938), pp. 303-11. The text of *La Création* is to be found in Réaume and Caussade, III, 325-444; hereafter cited as *CR*.

4. (Paris, Lucas Breyer). For text see Réaume and Caussade, III, 315-24; hereafter cited as *V*.

5. Consult H. Chamard, *Histoire de la Pléiade* (Paris, 1940), III, 212-14.

6. Réaume and Caussade, III, 207-70; hereafter cited as *PD*.

7. For text see Réaume and Caussade, IV, 313-24 and the edition by Weber, pp. 347-58; hereafter cited as *Di*.

8. See Réaume and Caussade, IV, 327-79. Extracts are also given in the Weber edition, pp. 335-46.

9. Réaume and Caussade, IV, 381-87; hereafter cited as *PE,* Roman numerals refer to poem numbers.

Selected Bibliography

PRIMARY SOURCES

1. Published Sources

Les Avantures du Baron de Faeneste. Au Dezert, 1630. The first complete edition; Books I and II appeared in 1617 and Book III in 1619.
Histoire universelle. 3 vols. Maillé: Jean Moussat, 1616, 1618, 1620.
Oeuvres. Edited by H. Weber, J. Bailbé, and M. Soulié. Paris: Gallimard, 1969. Reprints the main works but only extracts of minor collections of verse. An excellent edition with comprehensive bibliography.
Oeuvres complètes. 6 vols. Edited by E. Réaume and F. de Caussade. Paris: A. Lemerre, 1873–1892. Contains the vast majority of literary output with notable exception of the *Histoire universelle.*
Pages inédites. Edited by Pierre-Paul Plan. Geneva, Société d'histoire et d'archéologie, 1945. A transcription of previously unpublished correspondence, Latin verse, and other poems.
Petites oeuvres meslées. Geneva, Pierre Aubert, 1630. Includes "The Meditations on the Psalms," "L'Hyver," and other diverse poems.
Le Printemps. L'Hécatombe à Diane et les Stances. Edited by Henri Weber. Paris: Presses Universitaires de France, 1960.
Le Printemps: Stances et Odes. Edited by F. Desonay. Geneva: Droz, 1952.
Les Tragiques, donnez au public par le larcin de Promethee, Au dézert, par L.B.D.D., 1616.
Les Tragiques. Edited by I. D. McFarlane. London: Athlone Press, 1970. A selection with an important introduction.

2. Manuscripts

Geneva. Bibliothèque Publique et Universitaire. Collection Tronchin. Vols. 151–161.

SECONDARY SOURCES

"AGRIPPA D' AUBIGNÉ." *Europe* 54, No. 563 (1976). A series of studies of d'Aubigné and mainly connected with *Les Tragiques.*
BAILBÉ, JACQUES. *Agrippa d'Aubigné, poète des Trqgiques.* Caen: Faculté des Lettres et Sciences Humaines de l'Université de Caen, 1968. A rigorous analysis of thesis dimensions.

BUFFUM, IMBRIE. *Agrippa d'Aubigné's "Les Tragiques"*. *A study in the baroque style in poetry.* New Haven: Yale University Press, 1951. Underlines stylistic similarities between *Les Tragiques,* the plastic arts, and other contemporary works.

GARNIER, ARMAND. *Agrippa d'Aubigné et le parti protestant, contribution à l'histoire de la Réforme en France.* 3 vols. Paris: Fischbacher, 1929. Essential for d'Aubigné's life and the historical context. Some dates can be challenged but still valid introduction.

HAGIWARA, M. P. *French Epic Poetry in the Sixteenth Century.* The Hague: Mouton, 1972. Replaces *Les Tragiques* in their literary and historical context.

JEANNERET, MICHEL. "Les Styles d'Agrippa d'Aubigné." *Studi Francesi* 52 (1967), 246–57. Studies the Psalm translations.

MORRISON, IAN R. "'Paraître' and 'être.' Thoughts on d'Aubigné's 'Avantures du baron de Faeneste.'" *Modern Language Review* 68 (1973), 762–70. Interesting insight into the comic style.

PLATTARD, JEAN. *Agrippa d'Aubigné. Une figure de premier plan dans nos lettres de la Renaissance.* Paris: Boivin, 1931. Good short introduction to man and his work.

REGOSIN, RICHARD L. *The poetry of inspiration; Agrippa d'Aubigné's Les Tragiques.* Chapel Hill: University of North Carolina Press, 1970. Examines link between *Les Tragiques,* the *Apocalypse,* and Bullinger's commentary on the latter.

SAUERWEIN, HENRY A. *Agrippa d'Aubigné's "Les Tragiques"*. *A Study in structure and poetic method.* Baltimore: Johns Hopkins Press, 1953. Good and stimulating structural analysis.

WEBER, HENRI. *La Création poétique au XVIe siècle en France. De Maurice Scève à Agrippa d'Aubigné.* 2 vols. Paris: Nizet, 1956. A section devoted to *Les Tragiques* provides a sensitive appraisal of its literary qualities.

——. "Structure et langage dans 'Les Avantures du baron de Faeneste.'" In *De Jean Lemaire de Belges à Jean Giraudoux Mélanges d'histoire et de critique littéraire offerts à Pierre Jourda,* edited by E. Bouvier, pp. 111–30. Paris: Nizet, 1970.

Index

Alexander VI, Pope, 108
Amboise, Conspiracy of, 11, 18
Amboise, François d', 32
Arza, Loys d', 13
Asnières, duke of, 13
Aubigné, Agrippa d', *Les Avantures du Baron de Faeneste,* 14, 46, 54, 82-103, 118, 155; *Le Caducée,* 115-20; *La Confession du sieur de Sancy,* 83, 95, 97, 104-14, 118, 148, 149, (*Les Avis de Luat, 107*); *La Création,* 142-43; *Discours par Stances,* 45, 147-48; *Le Divorce satyrique,* 114-15, 118, 120; *Du Debvoir mutuel des Roys et des subjects,* 51, 121-24, 126, 148; *L'Hercule chrétien,* 43; *Histoire universelle,* 14, 39, 45, 82, 83, 97, 118, 124, 126; *L'Hiver,* 19, 140-42; *Lettre à Madame sur la douceur des afflictions,* 57; *Lettres sur diverses sciences,* 138; "Meditations on the Psalms," 48, 128-37; *Petites OEuvres meslées,* 128, 138; *Poésies diverses,* 144-47; *Le Printemps,* 17-37, 40, 140, 145, 155; "Religious verse", 138-43; *Sonnets et pièces épigrammatiques,* 148-53; *Les Tragiques,* 14, 16, 19, 20, 38-81, 83, 97, 98, 101, 109, 118, 124, 126, 130, 134, 135, 136, 139, 142, 148, 155; *Misères,* 48-50, 108, 129, 147, 149; *Princes,* 51-53, 92, 108, 129, 149; *La Chambre dorée,* 36, 53-55, 96; *Les Feux,* 55-58; *Les Fers,* 58-62; *Vengeances,* 62-64, 96; *Jugement,* 65-68, 132; *Traité sur les Guerres Civiles,* 124-27; *Vers funebres sur la mort de Jodelle,* 143-44
Aubigné, Constant d', 14
Aubigné, Jean d', 11
Aubigné de la Fosse, Nathan d', 15, 142

Baïf, Antoine de, 138
Bèze, Théodore de, 15, 128, 133; *Abraham Sacrifiant,* 19, 41; *Juvenilia,* 20, 41; "Psalms", 135
Bosch, Hieronymous, 65
Bouchet, Guillaume, *Les Serées,* 79
Bourbon, Cardinal de, 105
Boyssières, Jean de, *Troisiesmes OEuvres,* 19, 30
Burlamachi, Rénee, 15

Calvin, Jean, 15, 42, 97; *Institution chrétienne,* 70, 97
Calvinism, 48, 142
Catherine de Medici, 49-50, 52, 70, 72, 75
Cayet, Palma, 91
Cervantes, *Don Quixote,* 86, 100, 102; *Novales Exemplares,* 102
Charles IX, 51, 60, 70, 74, 122, 149, 150
Châtel, Jean, 46, 50
Clément, Jacques, 112, 122
Colligny, Amiral de, 74
Concini, Marquis, 91
Condé, Prince of, 82, 92
Corneille, Thomas and Donneau de Visé, *La Devineresse,* 91
Cotton, Father, 14, 97, 151
Crescentio, Marcel, 64
Crespin, Jean, *Histoire des martyrs,* 55, 107

Desportes, Philippe, 28, 30, 105; *Amours de Diane,* 20, 23
Domitian (Emperor), 71, 96
Du Bartas, Guillaume, 97; *La Semaine,* 40, 142
Du Bellay, Joachim, 36, 152; *La Deffence et Illustration de la Langue françoyse,* 40; *Les Antiquitez,* 49
Duelling, 50, 89
Du Fail, Noël, 85

167

Du Perron, Jacques, 14, 97, 105, 106, 112, 113, 149
Du Perron, Jean, 106, 112
Du Plessis-Mornay, Philippe, 97, 105, 116, 117, 118, 128, 133; *Vindiciae contra tyrannos,* 121

Edict of Nantes, 14, 115, 126
Elizabeth I of England, 55, 104
Epernon, duke of, 82, 92
Erasmus, Desiderius, 43, 85
Estienne, Henri, 85, 119
Estrées, Gabrielle d', 104, 109

Garnier, Robert, 42
Goulard, Simon, 16

Hadrian (Emperor), 71, 96
Henry III, 31, 38, 51, 52, 61, 72, 76, 104, 110, 112, 123, 149
Henry IV, 11, 12, 13, 14, 36, 38, 46, 50, 65, 86, 89, 90, 104, 107, 108, 109, 111, 112, 114-15, 116, 117, 129, 132, 133, 147-48, 154
Herod, 63
Hesteau de Nuysement, Clovis, 30
Homer, 68
Hotman, François, *Franco-Gallia,* 121

Journée des Barricades, 61
Julian the Apostate (Emperor), 64, 71, 96, 108

La Boétie, Etienne, *Discours sur la Servitude volontaire,* 121
La Jessée, Jean de, 30
La Meschinière, Pierre de, 30
La Noue, Odet de, 138
La Taille, Jean de, *Saül le furieux,* 42
The League, 95, 98, 122
Le Caron, Louis, 85
Le Duchat, Jacob, 103
Le Jeune, Claude, 138
Lesdiguières, Maréchal de, 125, 154
L'Estoile, Pierre de, 108, 152
Lezay, Suzanne de, 14, 20, 133-34, 138
Libanius, 97
Liberius (Pope), 97
Lorraine, Cardinal of, 49-50, 70

Louis XIII, 38, 98, 102, 125, 129, 147, 154
Loyola, Ignatius, 41, 125, 147

Maillard, Olivier, 94
Marguerite de Navarre, 83, 85
Marguerite de Valois, 30, 31, 33, 52, 114-15
Marie de Medici, 14, 83, 87, 98, 114, 116, 124, 147-48
Marot, Clément, 24, 135, 145
Mérimée, Prosper, 103
Mérindol, 64
Monistrol, Chassanion de, *Des Grands et Redoutables Jugemens et Punitions de Dieu,* 70
Montaigne, *Essais,* 39, 45, 52, 54, 79, 109

Nérac, 29-30
Nero, 64, 71, 96

Ovid, 28, 145

Paul IV (Pope), 63
Petrarch, 22, 31, 55, 95
Petrarchism, 22, 23, 24, 25, 31, 35, 36, 75, 145
Philip II of Spain, 63
Philip IV of Spain, 102
Plato, 31
Pléiade, 21, 40, 41, 48, 49, 68, 129, 144, 145
Poupo, Pierre, *La Muse chrestienne,* 20

Rabelais, 54, 83, 84, 85, 86, 99, 100, 108, 151
Rapin, Nicolas, 138
Ravaillac, François, 46, 147
Régnier, Mathurin, 36
Ripa, Cesare, *Iconology,* 79
Ronsard, Pierre de, 20, 22, 30, 37, 44, 45, 49, 129, 145; *Amours de Marie,* 21; *Discours sur les misères de ce temps,* 40; *La Franciade,* 40, 68-69; *Institution pour l'Adolescence du Roy,* 52; *Livret de folastries,* 36; *Sonnets pour Hélène,* 23, 36; *Sur la mort de Marie,* 31

Index

Rotan, Jean-Baptiste, 105

St Bartholomew's Day Massacre, 13, 17, 39, 47, 60, 63, 74, 77, 96, 104, 114, 122, 126
St Cyprian, 58
St Teresa, 41
Ste Marie du Mont, Baron of, 106-107, 108
Salviati, Diane, 13, 17-37, 40
Salviati, Jean, 17-18
Satire Ménippée, 95, 113, 119
Seneca, 70, 98
Socrates, 119, *Crito,* 12
Sourdis, Cardinal de, 109

Sponde, Jean de, 40, 105, 106, 109, 112, 128
Sully, duke of, 105, 107

Tahureau, Jacques, 85, 119
Thomas, Artus, *L'Isle aux Hermaphrodites,* 54
Tronchin, Théodore, 15, 148
Tyard, Pontus de, *Solitaire premier,* 46

Virgil, 68, 69
Voltaire, 113

Yver, Jacques, 85